BIBLE
STORIES *for*
GEN Z — *Teens in a*
MODERN WORLD

OLD & NEW TESTAMENT

Olive Branch Publishing

Olive Branch

P U B L I S H I N G

TABLE OF CONTENTS

—————————————— NEW TESTAMENT ——————————————

Introduction

Welcome to "Bible Stories for Gen Z Teens in a Modern World!", where ancient wisdom meets modern life. Picture this: you're taking age-old stories and remixing them into your daily playlist, making them as relevant as your latest Instagram post or your last Snapchat. When I was a teen, I found the Bible to be a maze of stories—deep and intricate, yet hard to navigate and understand. As I grew older and had children of my own, remembering this struggle helped spark my mission: to translate these epic tales into *your* language, connecting dots from millennia ago straight to here and now.

For Teens:

Imagine if your life's moments—whether you're taking a test, facing drama with friends, or just hanging out—had echoes from the past that could guide you today. That's what you'll find here. We've spun the tales of Noah, Moses, Jesus, the Apostles, Paul, and more, into something you can vibe with. These aren't your average stories; they're life hacks from history, designed to sync with *your* reality. Whether you're dealing with friend feuds, not making the team, or just plain figuring out who you want to be, there's a story here that mirrors your struggle and shines a light on your next move.

For Parents and Educators:

You're the coaches, the MVPs in the lives of these young adults. This book isn't just a retelling of ancient tales—it's a conversation starter, a bridge that links timeless wisdom to the TikTok generation. Each chapter is crafted to help you guide your teens through life's puzzles, providing a backdrop to discuss everything from ethics to personal challenges, all in a language that resonates with them.

Why the Bible?

These narratives have stood the test of time, not merely as religious texts but as a playbook of human experiences—our battles with right and wrong, the ripple effects of our choices, and our universal quest for purpose. In reimagining these stories, I've aimed to craft each one as a lens through which we can view our own lives, discovering timeless truths that still make sense in our fast-paced world.

Let's decode these ancient scripts together, finding clues for handling today's challenges and lighting up your path to adulthood. Here's to connecting dots from the past in ways that light up your present and future!

THE OLD TESTAMENT

CHAPTER 1
THE SYMPHONY OF
CREATION

(Genesis 1-2)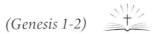

In the beginning, there was nothing—a canvas of infinite possibilities, waiting for a touch of divine creativity. Then, God spoke into the void, His voice resonating through the emptiness like the sickest beat drop.

God: "Let there be light."

And boom, light flooded the cosmos, slicing through the darkness, creating day and separating it from night. This brilliant beginning marked the first day of a masterpiece in the making (Genesis 1:1-5).

On the second day, God crafted an expanse called the sky, a vast blue canvas that divided the waters below from the waters above.

God: "Let there be a vault between the waters to separate water from water."

This division set the stage for life, a backdrop as breathtaking as any viral sunset pic you've seen on Instagram (Genesis 1:6-8).

Day three rolled around, and God turned His attention to the earth.

God: "Let the land produce vegetation: seed-bearing plants and trees on the land that bear fruit with seed in it, according to their various kinds."

Picture every plant and tree springing to life, a lush explosion of green, like the world's most epic botanical garden, only wilder and perfectly balanced (Genesis 1:9-13).

Come the fourth day, God didn't just hang lights in the sky; He set up an entire celestial system.

God: "Let there be lights in the vault of the sky to separate the day from the night, and let them serve as signs to mark sacred times, and days and years."

The sun ruled the day, a fiery leader, while the moon and stars took the night shift, crafting a rhythm of time, seasons, and navigation, predating any GPS tech (Genesis 1:14-19).

Day five added motion and life to the masterpiece. The waters and skies filled with creatures.

God: "Let the water teem with living creatures, and let birds fly above the earth across the vault of the sky."

From the majestic whales to the tiniest fish and birds painting the sky with their colorful wings, the world was now buzzing, a bustling scene of life and activity (Genesis 1:20-23).

On the sixth day, the grand finale:

God: "Let the land produce living creatures according to their kinds: livestock, creatures that move along the ground, and wild animals, each according to its kind."

The earth obeyed, and animals of all shapes and sizes roamed freely. But then, God had an idea for His masterpiece—humanity.

God: "Let us make mankind in our image, in our likeness, so that they may rule over the fish in the sea and the birds in the sky, over the livestock and all the wild animals, and over all the creatures that move along the ground."

So, humans were created, in God's image, to connect, rule, and care for the earth—a responsibility and a privilege (Genesis 1:24-31).

On the seventh day, God rested. He looked over the cosmos and saw that it was not just good; it was lit—it was everything it was meant to be. This pause was a divine example of balancing work and rest, an eternal vibe check for all of us (Genesis 2:1-3).

Why It Matters Today

Here's the takeaway for you: life can be overwhelming with school pressures, social life, and that constant stream of social media notifications. The story of the Creation teaches us about balance—the importance of pacing our responsibilities and finding time to recharge. It's like how each day of the Creation had its own purpose, reminding us to appreciate the process rather than rush.

Imagine, even God, in His infinite power, rested on the seventh day, emphasizing the need to pause and appreciate our achievements. This isn't just about taking breaks; it's recognizing the importance of enjoying life's moments and understanding our role in caring for the world. Whether it's through recycling, volunteering, or saving energy, you have the power to make a positive impact.

It's about finding harmony in the chaos, taking care of your world and your relationships, and maybe taking a break to just breathe and appreciate the beauty around you.

Now, let's take this refreshed understanding into your everyday hustle: balance your studies with your downtime, engage with nature, and manage your digital life so you're not just living online but loving the real world too. That's how you make each day of your life as epic as the days of the Creation.

CHAPTER 2
THE GARDEN OF WHISPERS

(Genesis 2-3)

In the beginning, there was Eden—a place of sheer beauty, where every tree burst with life, and peace filled the air. Among these trees stood one that was especially significant: the Tree of the Knowledge of Good and Evil, a symbol of the boundaries set by the divine, marking the gravity of choice.

Adam and Eve lived in this tranquil paradise, roaming freely and joyfully amidst nature's splendor. They could feast on any fruit, except for one—the fruit from the Tree of the Knowledge of Good and Evil. This was the only off-limits command given by God, a test of their trust and obedience.

However, tranquility was disrupted by a sly visitor. The serpent, more cunning than any other wild animal, slithered into the scene with a deceptive question aimed at Eve.

Serpent: "Did God really say, 'You must not eat from any tree in the garden'?" (Genesis 3:1)

Eve: "We may eat from the trees in the garden, but God did say, 'You must not eat from the tree that is in the middle of the garden, nor may you touch it, or you will die.'" (Genesis 3:2-3)

Serpent: "You will not certainly die. For God knows that when you eat from it, your eyes will be opened, and you will be like God, knowing good and evil." (Genesis 3:4-5)

Swayed by the serpent's words and the allure of gaining wisdom, Eve reached out, took the fruit, and ate it. She also shared it with Adam, who was with her, and he too ate.

Immediately, their eyes were opened to their own nakedness; they felt exposed and scrambled to cover themselves with fig leaves. It was the first rush of shame, the initial crack in their innocence, as the weight of their disobedience dawned on them (Genesis 3:6-7).

As dusk approached and the cool winds began to stir, God called out to them, now hidden among the trees of the garden.

God: "Where are you?" (Genesis 3:9)

Adam: "I heard you in the garden, and I was afraid because I was naked; so I hid." (Genesis 3:10)

God: "Who told you that you were naked? Have you eaten from the tree that I commanded you not to eat from?" (Genesis 3:11)

Adam: "The woman you put here with me—she gave me some fruit from the tree, and I ate." (Genesis 3:12)

God to Eve: "What is this you have done?" (Genesis 3:13)

Eve: "The serpent deceived me, and I ate."

God then pronounced judgments on all involved—the serpent was cursed to crawl on its belly, Eve would face pain in childbirth and conflicting desires with her husband, and Adam was told that the ground was cursed because of his actions. Life would now involve toil and sweat to produce food from the earth (Genesis 3:14-19).

With that, they were banished from Eden, sent to toil on the land from which they were formed, forever reminded of the cost of breaking trust and the enduring impact of choices.

Why It Matters Today

Imagine you're facing a tough choice where the easier option might lead to immediate gratification—like peeking at a friend's test paper during an exam or bending the truth on social media to get more likes. Adam and Eve's story teaches us about the consequences of our actions, especially when we choose short-term gains over what we know is right.

Their experience in Eden isn't just an ancient story; it's a daily reality about facing our desires and the serpent-like temptations that whisper shortcuts and easyouts. Making the right choice often means taking the harder path, but it builds integrity and trustworthiness—qualities that define us far beyond our teenage years.

This story also teaches us about responsibility. Adam tried to shift the blame to Eve, and Eve blamed the serpent, but each of them had to face the consequences of their actions. It's a powerful reminder to take ownership of our decisions and their impacts on our lives and those around us.

So, the next time you're at a crossroads, remember Adam and Eve. Consider not just the immediate benefits but the long-term effects of your choices. Strive to make decisions that you can be proud of, that align with your values, and that reflect the person you aspire to be.

CHAPTER 3
CAIN AND ABEL:
A TALE OF TWO BROTHERS

(Genesis 4)

Back in the early days after creation, Adam and Eve raised two sons: Cain, the farmer, and Abel, the shepherd. Each brother was into his own gig, mastering the arts of farming and shepherding. When it came time to show some gratitude to God, they both brought offerings from their hard work.

Cain rolled up with some fruits of his labor—literally, fruits from the ground he tilled. Abel, on the other hand, brought the fat portions from some of the firstborn of his flock. Here's the twist: God was feeling Abel's offering but didn't show the same love for Cain's. It wasn't about the stuff they brought, but more about the vibe and intention behind it.

Cain was seriously bummed out and got super salty about it. His face was all kinds of downcast, and his heart started to brew a storm of anger and jealousy.

God to Cain: "Why are you tripping? If you do what's legit, won't you be accepted? But watch out, sin is like a creeper at your door, hungry to get you, but you've got to master it."

Despite the heads-up from God, Cain couldn't shake off his rage. He invited Abel out to the field and, in a dark twist, he lashed out and killed him—the first ever murder.

When God came around asking, "Where's your brother Abel?" Cain hit him with, "I don't know. Am I supposed to babysit my brother?" His cheeky response showed he was trying to dodge the blame. But God, who sees everything, wasn't fooled. He told Cain that from now on, he'd be a restless wanderer, disconnected from the earth that soaked up his brother's blood.

Even in dishing out the punishment, God wasn't heartless. Cain was freaking out, thinking someone would take him out for what he did. So, God marked Cain to protect him from any revenge attacks. That mark? It was a sign that justice and mercy could coexist, even in tough times.

Why It Matters Today

Cain and Abel's story resonates deeply today, highlighting how unchecked emotions like jealousy and anger can lead to disastrous consequences. It's a vivid reminder of the importance of managing our feelings and seeking healthy ways to express dissatisfaction or hurt without harming others.

This narrative also speaks to personal responsibility. Cain's question, "Am I my brother's keeper?" challenges us to consider our responsibilities towards one another. In a world where it's easy to feel disconnected, remembering our role in each other's lives is crucial—whether it's supporting a friend, standing up for a classmate, or simply being there for someone in need.

Moreover, God's response to Cain teaches us about accountability and the potential for redemption. Even when we falter, making choices that lead us astray, the path to redemption is always open through responsibility and repentance.

In your daily interactions, whether at school, online, or at home, remember that your actions have weight, and how you handle your emotions and responsibilities can shape not just your life but also those around you.

CHAPTER 4
NOAH'S UNWAVERING FAITH

(Genesis 6-9)

Long before TikTok trends and instant updates, the world was wild in a whole different way. Humanity's heart was loaded with wickedness, turning life on Earth into a chaotic mess. Amid this turmoil stood Noah, a rare example of goodness in a world run by bad vibes (Genesis 6:5-8).

God hit Noah with a major reality check one day:

God: "The end of all flesh is here because the earth is overrun with violence. I'm about to clean the slate. Build an ark out of gopher wood, deck it out with rooms, and waterproof it inside and out" (Genesis 6:13-14).

This project was epic—more than just a weekend DIY. Noah was tasked with building a massive ark that would save his family and a slice of every living species from a flood set to reset the planet.

Picture Noah, spending day after day building this massive ark nowhere near water. His neighbors probably thought he was off his rocker.

Neighbor: "Hey Noah, why the giant boat, dude? Expecting the world to flood or something?"

Despite the side-eyes and whispers, Noah's faith never shook. He knew the stakes and stuck to the plan, following God's blueprints to the letter. His dedication was a silent shout about sticking to your guns, even when everyone else thinks you're crazy (Genesis 6:22).

Then, it all went down. The sky turned dark, and it started pouring like never before. The familiar world washed away, leaving Noah's ark riding the waves of a total reboot (Genesis 7:10-24).

Months later, the water chilled out. The ark parked on the mountains of Ararat, and a new game began. Noah and his crew stepped into a fresh world, a clean slate where second chances were legit.

God: "Here's the deal—I'm setting up a covenant with you. Never again will a flood do a total wipeout on earth" (Genesis 9:11).

God threw a rainbow across the sky as a sign-off on this promise, a shout-out to peace and fresh starts.

Why It Matters Today

Noah's story isn't just about survival—it's about standing firm in your beliefs, even when faced with skepticism or outright mockery. It's about doing what's right, not what's easy or popular. Think about how often we face peer pressure, whether it's about following a trend, cheating on a test, or joining in on a joke at someone else's expense.

Like Noah, choosing a different path can feel lonely. It can seem as though you're building your own 'ark'—maybe sticking up for a classmate, dedicating yourself to a cause, or simply choosing integrity over convenience. But remember, like the rainbow after the rain, there is always hope and renewal on the other side of hardship.

Noah's story teaches us about resilience and the importance of being true to oneself and one's values, no matter the storm you face. Let this be a reminder that the choices you make can steer your life towards new horizons, just as Noah steered his ark towards a new beginning.

CHAPTER 5
THE TOWER OF BABEL:
A LESSON IN LIMITS

(Genesis 11)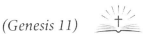

Not long after Noah's descendants began to multiply and spread across the earth, humanity was united with one language and a common goal. They settled in a plain in Shinar and cooked up a plan to make a serious mark. It wasn't just any project; they aimed to build a city and a tower so tall it would reach the heavens. But this was more than just constructing a monument; they wanted to make a name for themselves and avoid being scattered all over the world.

The people: "Come, let's build ourselves a city, with a tower that reaches to the heavens, so that we may make a name for ourselves; otherwise, we will be scattered over the face of the whole earth." (Genesis 11:4)

Driven by pride and a thirst for fame, they also sought to unify on their own terms, ignoring the intended diversity of life. They innovated with bricks instead of stone and used tar for mortar, marking their technological progress but also their ambition to create something permanent and grand.

God watched their efforts and the intentions behind them. Seeing that their unity could lead to even greater arrogance and self-dependence, He decided it was time to step in.

God: "If as one people speaking the same language they have begun to do this, then nothing they plan to do will be impossible for them. Come, let us go down and confuse their language so they will not understand each other." (Genesis 11:6-7)

Suddenly, communication broke down. People couldn't understand each other anymore, and the inability to communicate stopped the tower's construction in its tracks. The city was named Babel because that's where God mixed up the world's languages, causing everyone to scatter.

Why It Matters Today

The Tower of Babel story resonates with modern themes of ambition, teamwork, and the limits of human endeavor. It reminds us that while striving to achieve great things is admirable, the motives behind our actions matter immensely. When ambition is driven by pride or a desire to outdo others for personal glory, it can lead to unintended consequences.

This story also speaks to the power and pitfalls of communication. In today's digital age, where social media platforms allow us to "build towers" — crafting online personas and viral content to gain fame — the lesson of Babel remains relevant. Miscommunication and misunderstanding can easily occur, and while technology connects us, it can also divide.

Moreover, the scattering of Babel's builders reflects the challenges and beauty of diversity. It reminds us that embracing multiple perspectives and languages enriches our world, even if it sometimes complicates our interactions.

Babel's story encourages reflection on how we communicate, collaborate, and consider the ramifications of our ambitions. It invites you to build, not just to elevate yourself but to enhance and unify the community around you in meaningful ways.

Chapter 6
Abraham's Leap of Faith: A Journey to a Promised Land

(Genesis 12)

Abraham, then known as Abram, was chilling in Haran, a spot his family landed after moving from Ur of the Chaldeans. That's when God hit him up with a life-changing proposal that would not only redefine his life's path but also the history of many nations.

God to Abram: "Go from your country, your people, and your father's household to the land I will show you. I will make you into a great nation, and I will bless you; I will make your name great, and you will be a blessing." (Genesis 12:1-2)

This wasn't about just switching cities; it was a massive leap of faith—leaving everything familiar, like his home and culture, for some unknown territory. The promise was huge and packed with potential, but stepping into it required mad faith.

With incredible trust, Abram, at 75, instead of kicking back in retirement, chose to pack up for a nomadic adventure, responding to

God's call. He grabbed his wife Sarai, his nephew Lot, and all their stuff, and headed to Canaan.

Abram: "Let's roll. If this is where my journey's supposed to take me, I'm all in, even if I don't see the whole roadmap."

When they reached Canaan, God showed up again, giving Abram a thumbs up:

God: "To your offspring, I will give this land." (Genesis 12:7)

Abram built an altar there for the Lord, marking the spot as sacred, a bold move of devotion and thanks.

Sure, Abram's road was bumpy. There was a famine, pushing him to detour to Egypt to keep everyone fed. But through all the ups and downs, Abram's commitment to following God's vibe didn't waver. His life was a mix of fear, doubt, and some slip-ups, but the main story here is his steady faith and trust in what God promised.

Why It Matters Today

Abram's story is incredibly relevant to anyone standing on the brink of major life decisions—whether it's choosing a college, starting a new job, or moving out. Like Abram, you might feel that you're stepping into the unknown, faced with choices that involve leaving behind the familiar and embracing uncertainty.

His journey teaches us about the power of faith and the importance of being open to new possibilities, even when they seem daunting or unclear. It's about trusting in a greater plan for your life, one that may be beyond your current understanding.

Moreover, Abram's willingness to start anew, embracing a life of continual learning and adaptation, is a powerful model for personal growth. It shows that it's never too late to embark on a new path or to redefine who you are and what you contribute to the world.

As you face your "Canaan journeys," remember Abram's example. The paths we choose in response to our deepest callings can lead to profound blessings and opportunities, not just for ourselves but also for the communities and generations that follow.

CHAPTER 7
SODOM AND GOMORRAH: A TALE OF TWO CITIES

(Genesis 18-19)

Sodom and Gomorrah were notorious for their next-level wickedness, making them stand out for all the wrong reasons. The level of corruption was so high that it caught God's attention. Determined to see if the rumors matched reality, God planned a fact-finding mission to decide if these cities were beyond saving. Meanwhile, Abraham, who lived nearby, found himself in the middle of divine decision-making after God shared His plans.

God to Abraham: "The outcry against Sodom and Gomorrah is massive, and their sins are super serious. I'm going down to see if their actions really stack up to the complaints. If not, I'll know." (Genesis 18:20-21)

Worried about any decent folks who might still be living there, Abraham stepped up, diving into a gutsy negotiation with God, driven by his commitment to justice.

Abraham: "Are you going to wipe out the good with the bad? What if there are fifty righteous people in the city? Would you really sweep it away and not save it for the fifty good ones?" (Genesis 18:23-24)

Through a series of back-and-forths, Abraham hustled the number down from fifty to ten, hoping to save the cities based on the presence of just a few upright people. God was down for it, showing He was all about extending mercy.

Lot, Abraham's nephew, was chilling in Sodom with his family when two angels rolled into town to carry out the judgment. Lot convinced them to crash at his place. But soon, the city's dark side showed up big time. A mob surrounded Lot's house, demanding he hand over his guests.

Lot to the mob: "Don't do this vile thing. Look, I have two daughters who haven't been with anyone. I'll bring them out to you, and you can do what you want with them. But leave these guys alone; they're under my roof." (Genesis 19:6-8)

Things got intense until the angels stepped in, blinding the mob and telling Lot to grab his family and bail because the city's destruction clock was ticking.

Despite being told not to look back, Lot's wife glanced over her shoulder and turned into a pillar of salt, becoming a harsh symbol of disobedience. Lot and his daughters made it to the mountains, narrowly escaping the firestorm that obliterated Sodom and Gomorrah.

Why It Matters Today

The story of Sodom and Gomorrah isn't just ancient history— it's a deep dive into the ethics of society and the power of personal integrity, showing us how our collective choices shape our world.

This tale is clutch when you're figuring out how to navigate tricky situations like peer pressure or ethical dilemmas. It underlines the need to make choices that resonate with values like kindness, justice, and respect. Whether it's deciding how to treat your classmates, engaging online, or responding to unfairness, the lessons here are super relevant.

Plus, Abraham's actions show the importance of stepping up for others. His willingness to negotiate for the cities underscores our duty to seek justice and mercy, not just for ourselves but for our community. His readiness to engage in tough dialogues and advocate for the marginalized highlights that sometimes, like Abraham, your voice can seriously tilt the scales towards fairness and compassion in your community.

Reflect on your environment—where can you be a force for positive change? Maybe you can defend someone's rights or lead discussions that promote equity. Like Abraham, your actions have the power to make a real difference.

CHAPTER 8
THE TEST OF FAITH:
ABRAHAM AND ISAAC

(Genesis 22)

Years after being promised by God that he would father a great nation, Abraham faced the ultimate test of his faith. God commanded him to take his son Isaac, the child through whom the promise was to be fulfilled, and offer him as a sacrifice on a mountain in Moriah.

God to Abraham: "Take your son, your only son, whom you love—Isaac—and go to the region of Moriah. Sacrifice him there as a burnt offering on a mountain I will show you." (Genesis 22:2)

The command was bewildering and heart-wrenching. Yet, Abraham obeyed, setting out early the next morning with Isaac, firewood, and the elements needed for the sacrifice. His resolve did not waver, even as they climbed the mountain together.

As they walked, Isaac, unaware of the details of God's command, noticed something amiss.

Isaac: "Father, we have the fire and the wood, but where is the lamb for the burnt offering?" (Genesis 22:7)

Abraham: "God himself will provide the lamb for the burnt offering, my son." (Genesis 22:8)

Abraham's response, filled with faith and hope, masked the turmoil beneath. He prepared the altar, arranged the wood, and bound Isaac. As he raised the knife, his faith was palpable, poised between duty and despair.

At that critical moment, an angel of the Lord called out from heaven, stopping Abraham just in time.

Angel: "Do not lay a hand on the boy. Do not do anything to him. Now I know that you fear God, because you have not withheld from me your son, your only son." (Genesis 22:12)

A ram caught in nearby bushes was then provided as the offering, sparing Isaac. This test reaffirmed Abraham's unwavering faith in God's goodness and provision.

The altar on Moriah became a site not of loss but of profound divine provision. This story solidified Abraham's legacy and set a foundational example of faith and obedience for future generations.

Why It Matters Today

In your life, you might not face challenges as dramatic as Abraham's, but you'll encounter moments where you must decide between what is easy and what is right. This could be choosing to prioritize your long-term goals over immediate pleasures, like studying for an important exam instead of going out with friends, or it could be about standing up for what you believe in, even when it's unpopular or difficult.

This story also speaks to the concept of sacrifice in a modern context. Sacrifice today might mean dedicating time to help others, giving up personal gains for the greater good, or putting aside personal biases to understand and support someone else's struggles. These are the moments that test your character and shape who you are becoming.

Moreover, Abraham's faith that "God will provide" can be seen in how you might approach your own challenges with a mindset of hope and positivity. Believing that solutions will present themselves, that hard work will pay off, or that doing the right thing will lead to the right outcome is a powerful way to navigate life's complexities.

Reflect on your own experiences where you've had to make difficult choices. Consider how these moments are shaping your journey, just as Abraham's trial on Mount Moriah defined his. Think about how you can apply the lessons of faith, sacrifice, and moral courage in your everyday decisions.

This reimagined connection to the tale of Abraham and Isaac encourages you to recognize and appreciate the growth that comes from facing and overcoming the challenges in your life, reinforcing your personal values and the impact of your choices on your future.

CHAPTER 9
JACOB'S LADDER:
A STAIRWAY TO PURPOSE

(Genesis 28)

Fleeing from his brother Esau's wrath after snagging the blessing meant for the firstborn, Jacob was solo and feeling pretty exposed as night crept in. Needing a spot to crash, he picked a random place, making a makeshift pillow out of a stone under the open sky. What seemed like just another rough night on the road turned into a mind-blowing spiritual experience.

Jacob, settling down for the night: "Guess this spot will have to do. At least I've got the stars for company."

As Jacob crashed out, he dreamt of something wild—a ladder stretching from earth to heaven with angels going up and down on it. And up top? The Lord Himself was there, laying down some serious future plans.

God to Jacob: "I am the Lord, the God of your father Abraham and Isaac. This land you're lying on? It's yours. Your descendants will be as numerous as dust particles, spreading out in all directions. Through you and your offspring, everyone on earth will catch some blessings." (Genesis 28:13-14)

This vision wasn't just a promise of God having his back; it was a green light that the special family deal with Abraham was still on, now passed down to Jacob.

Waking up, Jacob was totally shook by realizing he'd just crashed at a divine hotspot, a literal "gate of heaven."

Jacob: "Wow, God was right here, and I didn't even know it. This place is incredible! It's nothing less than God's house; this is the gate of heaven." (Genesis 28:16-17)

Moved by the whole vibe, Jacob turned that ordinary stone into a sacred marker and poured oil on it, vowing that if God stuck by him, kept him in one piece on this crazy journey, then he'd stick by God too.

Why It Matters Today

In today's turbo-charged world, where you're sweating over picking the right career, acing your exams, or making massive life calls, Jacob's ladder is like a metaphor for finding direction and backup when you feel totally lost. It's about being open to those unexpected signs and breakthroughs that can clear up your path and choices.

This tale also shines a light on spotting the sacred spaces in our lives—those special spots or moments that feel extra significant or transformative. For Jacob, it was just a random place that turned into a profound meeting spot with the divine. For you, it could be anywhere you feel peace, get clarity, or feel connected—maybe that quiet corner in the library, your go-to community hangout, or even that online space where you vibe with support and positivity.

Plus, Jacob's way of honoring his epic vision—setting up that stone—teaches us about the power of commitment and making intentions real. You can mark important insights or decisions in your own life with personal rituals or symbols, like jotting down your goals, sharing your dreams with a mentor, or diving into volunteer work that lights you up, keeping you focused on your pledges and the support network you've got.

Jacob's story invites you to embrace and explore your own "ladder" moments—those pivotal experiences that deeply connect you to your bigger mission. It challenges you to stay alert to these divine meet-ups, use them as guides, and build on them as you push forward, just like Jacob did on his epic adventure.

CHAPTER 10
JOSEPH'S JOURNEY: FROM DREAMER TO DREAM MAKER

(Genesis 37, 39-47)

In Canaan, young Joseph was his dad's favorite, a status underscored by a dope coat of many colors—a gift that sparked serious envy among his brothers. Oblivious to the growing jealousy, Joseph didn't hold back on sharing his wild dreams.

Joseph: "Check this dream I had: We were out in the field tying up bundles of grain. Suddenly, my bundle stood up, while yours all gathered around and bowed down to it." (Genesis 37:6-7)

His brothers, already salty about his favored status, were not thrilled.

Brothers: "So, you think you're going to boss us around?" (Genesis 37:8 - paraphrased for narrative)

One day, as Joseph rolled up to check on them in the fields, they saw their chance to ditch "the dreamer." They chucked him into a pit and later, not pulling any punches, sold him into slavery. Carted off to Egypt, Joseph's dreams seemed like they were toast.

But in Egypt, Joseph's solid rep and skills caught the eye of Potiphar, one of Pharaoh's top guys. His hard work and honesty scored him a top spot in Potiphar's house, until a bogus charge got him tossed in jail. Even behind bars, Joseph's leadership mojo wasn't dimmed, and soon, he was running the show for all the prisoners.

While locked up, Joseph became known for his dream-decoding skills. Word got to Pharaoh, who was freaked by some confusing nightmares he had. Pulled before Pharaoh, Joseph laid it all out:

Joseph: "Pharaoh, your dreams are telling the same story. God's giving you the heads up: Egypt's about to have seven booming years of plenty, followed by seven brutal years of famine." (Genesis 41:25-30 - paraphrased for narrative)

Pharaoh was so impressed by Joseph's insight that he put him in charge of prepping Egypt for the famine.

When the famine hit hard, it wasn't just Egypt feeling the pinch—Canaan was reeling too. Joseph's own family came begging to Egypt for food, clueless that the governor they were dealing with was the brother they'd backstabbed.

The moment Joseph revealed who he was, the air was thick. But looking at the bigger picture, he chose to let bygones be bygones.

Joseph: "Don't beat yourselves up about selling me. God had a plan. He sent me ahead to save lives." (Genesis 45:5)

Joseph's rollercoaster—from dad's favorite to a slave, then a prisoner, and finally a top official—shows that life can flip in a heartbeat, but every twist and turn can build towards something epic.

Why It Matters Today

Joseph's story hits different when you think about your own challenges. Like him, you might find yourself blindsided by setbacks or drama that seem to throw off your game, but keeping your cool and staying positive can transform obstacles into launchpads.

Dealing with family issues, betrayal from buddies, or your own personal lows? Remember Joseph's power to forgive and find deeper meaning in his struggles. His saga pushes you to keep pushing forward, to leverage your unique strengths, and to stay open to patching things up and building anew, even when it's rough.

Rock your journey, knowing that like Joseph, you could be laying the groundwork for something major that only becomes clear later on. Stay loyal to your dreams, treat your tough times as chances to level up, and watch how your narrative influences those around you.

Chapter 11
Moses in the Bulrushes:
A Journey Begins

(Exodus 2)

In a time when the Hebrews in Egypt were crushed under severe oppression, a terrifying decree from Pharaoh mandated the death of every newborn Hebrew boy. Against this grim backdrop, a Levite woman gave birth to a son. Noticing her baby was exceptionally healthy, she hid him for three months. But as he grew, concealing him became unmanageable. Driven by desperation and hope, she hatched a plan.

Jochebed, Moses' mother: "I can't keep him hidden any longer, but there's no way I'm letting Pharaoh's soldiers find him."

She crafted a papyrus basket, sealed it with tar and pitch to waterproof it, and placed her son inside. Then, she tucked the basket among the reeds along the Nile River's bank, entrusting her child's fate to a higher power while her daughter, Miriam, kept watch from a distance.

Pharaoh's daughter came down to the river to bathe and noticed the basket nestled among the reeds. Curious, she sent her servant to retrieve it. When she opened the basket, she found the baby, crying. Her heart melted, pushing aside her father's cruel decree.

Pharaoh's daughter: "This must be one of the Hebrew babies."

Despite being fully aware of her father's command, she chose to save the child.

Seizing the opportunity, Miriam approached Pharaoh's daughter and proposed a savvy solution that would not only save her brother but also bring him back to their mother for his early upbringing.

Miriam: "Do you want me to find a Hebrew woman to nurse the baby for you?"

Pharaoh's daughter: "Yes, go."

Miriam quickly brought their mother, who was then hired by Pharaoh's daughter to nurse Moses. She even paid her wages, not knowing the nurse was actually the baby's biological mother.

Moses grew up straddling two worlds. Raised in Pharaoh's palace as an Egyptian prince, his roots remained firmly in the Hebrew community. This dual identity shaped his destiny, forging him into a bridge between his people and their oppressors, and ultimately, their liberator.

Why It Matters Today

Moses' story kicks off with acts of incredible bravery and compassion, showing how critical choices can change life's direction. Today, this tale underscores the power of individual actions, especially against the backdrop of injustice. Whether it's defending a classmate, pushing for change in your community, or aiding someone in need, your actions can create waves.

The narrative also emphasizes the importance of identity and the challenges it often brings. Like Moses navigating different communities and expectations, you might find yourself balancing diverse cultural or social realms. Embracing all facets of your identity and using your unique position to promote understanding and unity can be impactful.

Lastly, the story of Moses in the bulrushes is about protection and providential care. It reminds us that sometimes, the toughest choices—like Jochebed's decision to set Moses adrift on the Nile—are spurred by hope for a brighter future. It encourages you to stay hopeful and proactive in shaping your destiny, believing in the ripple effects of your courageous decisions.

CHAPTER 12
THE PLAGUES OF EGYPT:
A DIVINE CHALLENGE

(Exodus 7-12)

M oses, tapped by God to free the Israelites, rolled up on Pharaoh with a message that was straight-up divine. With his his crew and Aaron by his side, Moses dropped God's command like a boss.

Moses to Pharaoh: "Here's the word from the Lord, the God of Israel: 'Let my people go, so they can throw me a festival in the wilderness.'" (Exodus 5:1)

Pharaoh's clapback was full of shade and stubbornness.

Pharaoh: "And who's the Lord that I should obey him and let Israel go? I don't know the Lord, and I'm not letting Israel go." (Exodus 5:2)

As Pharaoh got all stubborn, God unleashed a mixtape of catastrophic plagues, each one a show of His power and Pharaoh's hardheadedness.

1. <u>Plague of Blood.</u> Aaron rocked his staff over Egypt's waters, turning all water into blood. Fish kicked the bucket, rivers stank, and the Egyptians couldn't sip a drop.

2. <u>Plague of Frogs.</u> With a flick of his hand over the rivers, Aaron called up frogs that crashed every Egyptian pad, hopping into ovens and bowls. Pharaoh teased them with freedom, only to ghost them once the frogs bounced.

3. <u>Plague of Gnats.</u> At Aaron's snap, dust transformed into gnats that partied on all people and animals. Egypt's magicians tried to copy this and failed, admitting, "This is the finger of God!"

4. <u>Plague of Flies.</u> Flies partied hard in Pharaoh's palace and his officials' cribs, leaving the Israelites' zone, Goshen, untouched, showing who was boss.

5. <u>Plague on Livestock.</u> A deadly pestilence ghosted Egyptian livestock chilling in the fields, but the Israelites' animals? They were all good.

6. <u>Plague of Boils.</u> Moses and Aaron threw down some furnace soot, causing boils to pop up on Egyptians and their animals.

7. <u>Plague of Hail.</u> Moses called down hail mixed with fire that wrecked Egypt's green scene. Pharaoh owned up to his mess but went back to his old ways once the hail dipped.

8. <u>Plague of Locusts.</u> On Moses' cue, a wind rolled through with locusts that munched on whatever survived the hail, cramming into houses and darkening the skies.

9. <u>Plague of Darkness.</u> Moses threw some shade, literally, stretching out his hand to blanket Egypt in darkness for three days, while Goshen stayed lit.

10. <u>Death of the Firstborn.</u> The real heavyweight hit at midnight, taking down every Egyptian firstborn, from regular folks to Pharaoh's own son, and that's what finally broke Pharaoh.

Pharaoh to Moses: "Bounce, take your people and your animals! Just go!"

Before the final smackdown, Moses had the Israelites mark their doorposts with lamb's blood, which told the angel of death to pass on by. This boss move turned into Passover, celebrating how they dodged disaster and got divine protection.

Why It Matters Today

The story of the Ten Plagues isn't just some old-school drama; it's about sticking it out and the power of staying strong against the odds. Like Moses throwing down with Pharaoh, you might find yourself in spots where you gotta stand up again and again for what you believe in, be it at school, in your community, or at a job. The plagues show that change might drag its feet, but staying on your grind can break through the biggest barriers.

This tale also big-ups resilience. Each hurdle you clear can beef up your spirit, much like the Israelites who leveled up with each challenge.

Think about the "plagues" in your life—what's tripping you up? How can you face them down with courage and keep pushing? Let Moses' saga pump you up to take those small, steady steps that lead to huge shifts, proving that even tough obstacles can be taken down with enough heart and hustle.

CHAPTER 13
THE PARTING OF THE RED SEA: A PATH THROUGH PERIL

(Exodus 14)

After finally being let go by Pharaoh, the Israelites, led by Moses, booked it out of Egypt. But their taste of freedom didn't last long. Pharaoh, hit with major regret and anger, chased after them with his army, cornering the Israelites between his squad and the Red Sea. Seeing the danger roll up, the Israelites freaked out.

The Israelites to Moses: "Seriously, Moses? Were there no graves in Egypt, so you brought us out here to die? Why'd you drag us out of Egypt?" (Exodus 14:11)

Moses, keeping his cool, reassured everyone.

Moses to the people: "Chill, everyone. Stand firm, and you'll see the epic save the Lord is about to pull off today. The Egyptians coming at us? You won't even see them tomorrow. The Lord's got our backs; just watch." (Exodus 14:13-14)

As the Egyptian army closed in, Moses raised his hand over the sea as God told him to. God whipped up a strong east wind, parting the sea and turning it into dry land with towering walls of water on each side. The Israelites walked across the sea floor, a miraculous escape route right there.

Narration: "The waters were like walls to them on their right and on their left." (Exodus 14:22)

When the Egyptians tried to follow, God threw them into total chaos. He made the wheels of their chariots fall off, which seriously slowed them down.

At the crack of dawn, Moses waved his hand over the sea again, and the waters rushed back, swamping the chariots and horsemen—all of Pharaoh's army that had followed them into the sea got wiped out.

Narration: "The water flowed back and covered the chariots and horsemen—the entire army of Pharaoh that had followed the Israelites into the sea. None of them survived." (Exodus 14:28)

Why It Matters Today

The Parting of the Red Sea is all about breaking free and the power of keeping faith. It shows that when you're up against the wall with seemingly no way out, keeping the faith and stepping up can lead to mind-blowing results. Maybe you're facing something tough like family drama, school stress, or tricky friend situations.

This story also highlights how dope it is when people pull together during tough times—like Moses rallying his people. You can be that leader or that solid friend in your crew.

Think about your own 'Red Seas'—those massive challenges staring you down. Remember, sometimes you gotta make bold moves, backed by faith in yourself and your squad.

This retelling, aimed at keeping it real and relevant, is here to fire you up to tackle your challenges with guts and hope, showing that no challenge is too massive when you come at it together.

CHAPTER 14
THE TEN COMMANDMENTS:
FOUNDATIONS OF FAITH

(Exodus 20)

After the Israelites escaped from Egypt and crossed the Red Sea, they trekked through the desert to Mount Sinai. Here, the scene was straight out of a blockbuster movie: the mountain shook, smoke billowed, and God descended in a fiery spectacle. It was a sight that shook everyone at the base of the mountain.

God to Moses and the people: "I am the Lord your God, who got you out of Egypt, out of that grind of slavery."

Then, God laid down the Ten Commandments, rules not just meant to keep everyone in line but to shape a society rooted in justice and righteousness:

1. No other gods before Me: Keep it 100 with your spiritual game. Focus your loyalty solely on God.

2. No idols: Keep your worship real. Don't pour your heart into just any image or icon.

3. Do not misuse God's name: Drop God's name with respect, not just casually or in a rant.

4. Keep the Sabbath holy: Hit the pause button one day a week to chill and reflect spiritually.

5. Honor your parents: Show love and respect for your fam—it's foundational.

6. Do not murder: Life's sacred, so protect it.

7. Do not commit adultery: Stay true in your relationships; keep it real and honest.

8. Do not steal: Respect what's not yours.

9. Do not bear false witness: Keep it straight. Promote justice and trust by being truthful.

10. Do not covet: Keep your cool and avoid obsessing over others' stuff.

Moses relayed these commandments to the people, who were all in, committing to follow everything God laid out. Moses took it down in writing, and they sealed the deal with a sacrifice, marking their dedication to this fresh start.

Why It Matters Today

The Ten Commandments are more than just some ancient rules; they're about setting the foundation for ethical behavior and personal responsibility. In today's world, where you're always running into complex moral choices, these commandments are like your moral GPS:

» Respecting others' space and stuff could mean keeping out of your classmate's business or safeguarding their privacy.

» Being honest, even when it's tough, helps build a community where people trust each other.

» Taking a break to just be can be crucial in our non-stop world.

Each commandment pushes you to think about how your actions impact others and encourages you to work towards a community where fairness, respect, and kindness are at the forefront. Whether you're religious or not, these principles are key in discussions about ethics, values, and who you want to be.

CHAPTER 15
THE GOLDEN CALF:
A TEST OF FAITH

(Exodus 32)

While Moses was up on Mount Sinai, grabbing the Ten Commandments, the Israelites down below were getting antsy. Their leader was MIA longer than they expected, and they started to feel the FOMO, big time.

The people to Aaron: "Yo, make us some gods who can lead the way. As for Moses, the dude who got us out of Egypt, who knows what's happened to him?" (Exodus 32:1)

Aaron, who was supposed to keep things chill, got swept up in the crowd's demands.

Aaron: "Alright, everyone, pull off those gold earrings from your wives, your sons, and your daughters, and bring them here."

From all that bling, Aaron crafted a calf, flexing his skills but totally missing the mark on the no-idol rule.

Aaron: "These are your gods, Israel, who brought you up out of Egypt." (Exodus 32:4)

He even set up an altar in front of the calf and kicked off a festival to the Lord, trying to mix legit worship with total idolatry, which just confused everyone even more.

When Moses came back, tablets in hand, he was salty to see the calf and the wild party around it. In a rage, he smashed the tablets at the mountain's base—totally shook at how quickly the squad had ditched their promises.

Moses to Aaron: "What did these people do to you, that you led them into such a savage sin?" (Exodus 32:21)

Aaron tried to ghost his responsibility, playing down his part in the idol's creation, which just spotlighted the massive fail and its heavy consequences.

God was high key upset and ready to throw down wrath, but Moses stepped in, begging for mercy. Even so, the fallout was brutal: Moses told the Levites to handle business, and about three thousand dudes paid with their lives. This harsh scene underscored how serious their betrayal was.

Moses went back to God to smooth things over for the people's mistake, showing his solid commitment to his crew and their bond with God. The smashed tablets got replaced eventually, a sign that even with major screw-ups, there's room for a comeback.

.

Why It Matters Today

The story of the Golden Calf hits with real talk about leadership, dealing with peer pressure, and the weight of bad choices. It's a reminder to stay true to your goals, especially when things get shaky.

In today's vibe, this story warns against the lure of quick fixes or just rolling with the crowd without thinking. It makes you wonder about your own "golden calves"—maybe it's clout, cash flow, or other distractions that could trip you up from your real values.

Aaron's story is a callout to leaders to stay woke and not just cave to the hype. It's all about making choices that don't just look good now but are solid long-term.

Reflecting on this, you're invited to check how you handle pressure and uncertainty. It's about building up that resilience and integrity, making sure your moves line up with your deepest values and what's really good for you in the long run.

CHAPTER 16
BALAAM'S DONKEY: VOICES OF THE UNEXPECTED

(Numbers 22)

B alaam, a prophet with some serious clout, got a tempting offer from Balak, the king of Moab, who was sweating bullets over the Israelites camping next door. Balak was like, "These folks are everywhere, help me out here, curse them so I can maybe push them back."

Balak's message to Balaam: "A crowd has rolled out of Egypt; they're all over the place and right next to me. Come and drop a curse on them for me; maybe I can take them on and shoo them away." (Numbers 22:5-6)

But when God hit up Balaam at night, He was straight-up: "Don't go with these guys or throw any shade at the Israelites, they're blessed." Initially, Balaam kept it real, turning down Balak's cash and clout offer.

But then, when Balak sent some high-tier messengers, Balaam got caught up in the hype and asked God again. This time, God was like, "Fine, go, but only spit the words I give you." So, Balaam hit the road the next morning, riding his donkey, but he wasn't really in sync with God's vibe.

On the way, an angel of the Lord, invisible to Balaam but visible to his donkey, blocked the path three times. Each time, the donkey dipped, which got Balaam all heated, and he started beefing with his donkey.

Balaam to his donkey: "If I had a sword, I'd straight up end you right now." (Numbers 22:29)

After the third dodge, God flipped the script and let the donkey talk, which was lit.

Balaam's donkey: "Why you gotta be harsh and hit me these three times?" (Numbers 22:28)

God then let Balaam see the angel chilling in the road with a drawn sword, and the angel threw some shade, saying Balaam's path was reckless and the donkey just saved his life.

Angel of the Lord: "You're wilding out here. Your donkey peeped me and dodged me these three times. If she hadn't, you'd be gone, and she'd be chilling." (Numbers 22:32-33)

Feeling the weight of his mistakes, Balaam was shook and offered to bounce back, but the angel told him to keep going, making sure to only drop God's words. Balaam rolled up to Moab and ended up blessing Israel instead of cursing them, sticking to God's script despite his earlier trip-up.

Why It Matters Today

The story of Balaam and his donkey slaps with a reminder about the importance of listening to those unexpected truth bombs. Balaam's tale shows the risks of letting greed or the thirst for clout cloud your judgment, a lesson that's super relevant today with all the temptation to flex for the 'gram or chase paper over principles.

As you navigate stuff like peer pressure, staying legit in school, or the madness of social media, this story highlights sticking to your ethical guns and the fallout from sleeping on moral advice. It teaches that wisdom might roll up from the most random places or peeps, like a talking donkey dropping knowledge.

Reflect on the "donkeys" in your life—those wild, out-of-nowhere moments or folks who've schooled you. Embrace those chances to level up, recognizing that the realest wisdom often pops up where you least expect it.

CHAPTER 17
JOSHUA AND THE BATTLE OF
JERICHO: WALLS FALL DOWN

(Joshua 6)

As the Israelites approached Jericho, they faced what looked like an impossible barrier: towering walls enclosing the city. But Joshua, their leader, got some wild instructions from God that turned typical battle strategies on their head.

God to Joshua: "Check it out, Joshua, Jericho is yours for the taking—king, warriors, and all. March around the city once a day with all your soldiers for six days. Have seven priests with ram's horn trumpets lead the way in front of the Ark of the Covenant. On the seventh day, go around seven times, then let the priests blow their trumpets like there's no tomorrow." (Joshua 6:2-4)

Joshua passed along these divine tactics, and the Israelites got to stepping. For six days, they circled Jericho in total silence except for the trumpet sound, building suspense and maybe even messing with the minds of those inside.

On the seventh day, after their seventh lap, Joshua gave the signal.

Joshua: "Yell your lungs out! The Lord has hooked us up with the city!" (Joshua 6:16)

As the trumpets blasted and the Israelites shouted, something insane happened—the walls of Jericho just collapsed, like they were hit by an invisible wrecking ball. The Israelite army stormed in and took the city, just as God had promised.

Amid the chaos, Joshua didn't forget about Rahab, the local who had risked her neck to hide Israelite spies. Her crib, part of the city wall, miraculously stayed intact, and her fam was saved, all because she had the guts to help out and believe in their cause.

Why It Matters Today

The Jericho story isn't just some ancient siege tale; it's about the 'walls' you face in your own life—those big challenges that seem too tough to take on, whether they're about hitting your personal goals, sorting out relationship drama, or wrestling with inner doubts.

This story pumps up the value of grit and faith. Like the Israelites' march, sometimes your journey to overcoming obstacles isn't about going in guns blazing but sticking it out, being patient, and trusting the process.

It also shines a light on the strength of sticking together. The Israelites' win wasn't just because they had weapons; it was their unity and following a shared plan that made those walls tumble down. It's a solid reminder of how teamwork can break through even the toughest barriers.

Plus, Rahab's part in this shows that sometimes, the most unexpected people can be your biggest allies. It celebrates reaching across divides and recognizing that everyone has value.

Reflect on the 'Jerichos' in your life—those big, scary walls. Think about how sticking to your faith, being patient, and working together could be your game-changer, just like it was for Joshua and his crew.

Chapter 18
Gideon's Battle:
Strength in Few

(*Judges 7*)

G ideon was just a regular guy from the weakest clan in Manasseh, feeling like the underdog of underdogs. When God tapped him to free Israel from the Midianite bullies, Gideon was all, "Me? Really? How can I pull this off when I'm the least of the least?" (Judges 6:15)

But God was like, "I'm with you, and that's all you need to rock this." Amped up by God's pep talk and a few solid signs that this was legit, Gideon started gathering troops, thinking he'd need a massive squad to take on Midian.

God, however, flipped the script: "You've got too many homies here. If you win with this crowd, you'll think you did it all yourselves. Tell anyone who's scared to hit the road." (Judges 7:2-3) After that, 22,000 dudes bounced, leaving 10,000.

Still too many for God's plan. So, He set up a quirky test at the waterhole—only those who lapped water like dogs while staying alert made the cut. End result? Gideon's army was down to just 300 men.

With his lean team, Gideon snuck up on the Midianite camp at night. Each man was armed with just a trumpet, a jar, and a torch hidden inside the jar. At Gideon's signal, they blasted the trumpets, smashed the jars to reveal the torches, and shouted, "A sword for the Lord and for Gideon!" This full-on audio-visual assault freaked out the Midianites so much that they started slashing at each other in the chaos, handing Gideon and his mini-crew a massive win with barely a fight.

Why It Matters Today

Gideon's story is a hype reminder that real power doesn't always roll with numbers or flash. It's about having the right game plan and some serious faith in something bigger than yourself. Even with a small crew, you can pull off huge wins if you play it smart.

This is super relevant whether you're facing down finals, trying to win that championship game, or just dealing with life's regular rough patches. Gideon's victory shows you don't need all the resources in the world to succeed; sometimes, what you've got is plenty if you're clever and brave about it.

Also, take a look at your own "squad"—it's not about how many you have, but the realness and quality they bring to your life. It's all about those who stand with you when it's time to smash some jars and make some noise.

Think about the "Midianites" in your life—those giant challenges that seem unbeatable. Gideon's story pushes you to think outside the box and trust in your unique strengths. Sometimes, underestimating yourself is the only thing really standing in your way.

CHAPTER 19
SAMSON AND DELILAH:
STRENGTH AND BETRAYAL

(Judges 16)

Samson, blessed with superhuman strength by God, had one major flaw—his heart, easily swayed by love and desire. Delilah, the woman he loved, became the centerpiece in a Philistine plot to take him down. The Philistine leaders offered her a hefty sum to uncover the secret of Samson's strength.

Philistine leaders to Delilah: "Find out what makes him so strong, and how we can bring him down. For this, we'll each give you eleven hundred shekels of silver." (Judges 16:5)

Delilah took up the challenge and started to dig into Samson about the source of his power. Despite her persistence, Samson first threw her off with fake stories. But Delilah kept at it, mixing her nagging with appeals to his feelings for her.

Delilah to Samson: "How can you say you love me when you won't trust me? You've played me three times now without sharing the secret of your strength." (Judges 16:15)

Worn down by her constant pressure and moved by his feelings for her, Samson finally spilled the beans—his strength was tied to his uncut hair, a symbol of his vow to God as a Nazirite.

One night, as Samson slept with his head in her lap, Delilah called in a man to cut his hair, draining Samson of his divine strength. The Philistines then grabbed him, blinded him, and threw him in a Gaza prison, where he was forced to grind grain.

In the depths of despair, Samson's hair began to regrow. Eventually, during a major Philistine bash in the temple of their god Dagon, they brought out blind Samson to mock him. It was then that Samson reached out to God one last time.

Samson to God: "Sovereign Lord, remember me. Please, God, give me strength just once more, and let me take revenge on the Philistines for my eyes." (Judges 16:28)

Positioned between the temple's central pillars, Samson pushed with all his might, and the temple crumbled, crushing him and killing the Philistine rulers and many others. In his death, Samson struck a final blow against those who had betrayed and humiliated him.

Why It Matters Today

Samson's story is a poignant reminder of how personal vulnerabilities, especially in relationships, can lead to one's downfall if not managed wisely. For teens, this narrative underscores the importance of being cautious about whom you trust and being aware of the motives of others around you.

It also speaks to the consequences of giving in to temptations that might seem harmless but can have significant repercussions. Samson's experience encourages a reflection on the importance of staying true to one's principles and commitments, even under pressure.

Additionally, the story illustrates that even in moments of weakness and failure, opportunities for redemption and the ability to impact the world around us still exist. It encourages finding strength in adversity and using one's experiences, both good and bad, to foster resilience and determination.

CHAPTER 20
RUTH AND NAOMI:
A TALE OF DEVOTION AND
REDEMPTION

(Ruth 1-4)

The story kicks off with Naomi, her hubby Elimelech, and their two sons ditching Bethlehem for Moab because of a nasty famine back home. But luck wasn't on their side—Elimelech passed away, and Naomi's sons, who had married Moabite women Orpah and Ruth, also died within a decade, leaving the women on their own.

In a tough patriarchal society, being a widow was no joke. Naomi, hitting a real low, decided to head back to Bethlehem and suggested her daughters-in-law go back to their fams for a better shot at remarrying.

Naomi to Orpah and Ruth: "Head back to your moms' places. May the Lord hook you up with kindness like you've shown to your late hubbies and me." (Ruth 1:8)

Orpah, though tearful, took the advice and split. But Ruth? She wasn't having any of that. Her loyalty was next-level.

Ruth to Naomi: "Don't push me to bail on you. Wherever you go, I go; your crib is my crib. Your crew will be my crew, and your God, my God." (Ruth 1:16)

Landing in Bethlehem, Ruth wasn't about to sit around. She hit the fields to glean barley, hustling to keep Naomi and herself fed. Boaz, who owned the fields and was related to Naomi's late husband, noticed Ruth grinding away and was seriously impressed by her dedication.

Boaz to Ruth: "Everyone's been talking about how you've had Naomi's back since your man died—how you left everything you knew to roll with people you never met." (Ruth 2:11)

Naomi, always on the lookout, saw a golden chance in Boaz for Ruth's—and indirectly her own—security. She cooked up a plan for Ruth to catch Boaz's eye, hoping he'd be down to marry Ruth as a kinsman redeemer, keeping her late son's line going. Ruth followed through, and Boaz was all in, especially after the closer relative passed on the responsibility.

Boaz and Ruth tied the knot, and their union didn't just lock down a solid future for Ruth and Naomi—it also set the stage for their kid, Obed, who would be King David's granddad. Talk about a major link in the Biblical big leagues!

Why It Matters Today

Ruth and Naomi's saga is all about how fierce loyalty and pure kindness can open doors and secure your future. For you guys today, it's a shoutout to cherish and strengthen the bonds with your family and friends. These relationships can be your rock when times get tough.

Plus, Ruth stepping into the unknown with guts and hope is a powerful nod to the strength in embracing new starts, even when the path isn't clear.

And the whole redemption vibe with Boaz and Ruth throws a spotlight on how communities can lift each other up, stressing mutual respect and support.

Think about the "Naomis" and "Ruths" in your life—the ones who've had your back and those you've supported. Reflect on how you can keep that loyalty strong and be a beacon of kindness and support in your crew, building a network that's all about helping each other thrive.

CHAPTER 21
SAMUEL'S CALL: LISTENING AND RESPONDING

(1 Samuel 3)

Samuel was just a young boy serving under the priest Eli at Shiloh, sleeping in the temple near the sacred Ark of God, when something epic went down that would totally redefine his future.

Narrative: "Back then, hearing from the Lord was rare; visions weren't exactly dropping daily." (1 Samuel 3:1)

One night, while Samuel was catching some Z's, he heard someone call his name. He thought it was Eli, so he hustled over to him.

Samuel to Eli: "You rang?"

But Eli hadn't called him. After this mix-up happened three times, Eli caught on that it was the Lord trying to get through to Samuel.

Eli to Samuel: "Head back to bed, and if he calls again, hit him with, 'Speak, Lord, for your servant is listening.'" (1 Samuel 3:9)

Samuel went back and chilled, waiting. Sure enough, the voice called out again, "Samuel! Samuel!"

Samuel: "I'm all ears, go for it." (1 Samuel 3:10)

God then clued Samuel in on some heavy stuff about the future of Israel and the tough times ahead for Eli's family due to his sons' shady dealings. It was a lot for a kid to handle, but it kicked off Samuel's role as a prophet.

Narrative: "God stuck by Samuel as he grew, making sure his words weren't just empty air." (1 Samuel 3:19)

From that night, Samuel stepped up as a major prophet, respected from Dan to Beersheba. His rep was all about being dialed into God's frequency, ready to listen and act on the divine guidance he received.

Why It Matter's Today

Samuel's story hits home for teens because it's all about tuning into guidance, whether it's from your mentors, your folks, or that gut feeling inside. Like Samuel, you might sometimes wonder about the calls to action you hear in your life—whether to chase a dream, lend a hand, or stand up for what's right.

This story pumps you up to listen up in those quiet moments and lean on the wisdom of your own "Elis" who can help you figure things out. It shows that even if the message is tough, grabbing it and running with it can lead to some serious growth and finding your purpose.

Think about how you deal with advice and insights in your life. Are you all ears like Samuel? Do you spot the "Eli" figures around you who can help make sense of what you're going through? Reflect on how you can boost your ability to listen deeply, helping you catch the right direction and respond with bravery and an open heart

Chapter 22
David vs. Goliath:
The Battle of Belief

(1 Samuel 17)

In the Valley of Elah, tension was thick as the Israelite and Philistine armies squared off. The Israelite camp was buzzing with fear, especially when Goliath, a massive warrior from Gath, stepped up. Decked out in intimidating armor and booming challenges across the valley, he was a sight to behold.

Goliath: "Pick a man to square off against me. If he takes me down, we'll serve you. But if I drop him, you'll serve us." (1 Samuel 17:8-9)

Everyone, including King Saul, was shaking in their boots—nobody was stepping up to this challenge. Enter David, a young shepherd boy, who was just delivering food to his older brothers in Saul's camp.

David caught wind of Goliath's trash talk and instead of fear, he felt a spark of faith and a drive to act.

David: "Who does this dude think he is, dissing the armies of the living God?" (1 Samuel 17:26)

King Saul doubted David at first because of his youth and lack of battle chops. But David was like, "Look, I've taken on lions and bears to protect my sheep. The same God who had my back then will have it now against this Philistine."

David: "God saved me from claws and teeth; He'll save me from this big guy too." (1 Samuel 17:37)

Saul caved and offered David his own heavy-duty armor, but David wasn't about that life. It felt all wrong. He stuck to his trusted sling and snagged five smooth stones from a stream.

As David stepped up to Goliath, the giant mocked his youth and simple weapon.

Goliath: "Am I a dog that you come at me with sticks?" (1 Samuel 17:43)

But David didn't waver. His reply was all faith, no fear.

David: "You come at me with all your weapons, but I come at you in the name of the Lord Almighty, the God you've defied." (1 Samuel 17:45)

With a calm and steady hand, David swung his sling and let loose one of the stones. It zipped through the air in a perfect arc, smacking Goliath right in the forehead. The giant toppled face-first into the dirt, knocked out by a kid armed with nothing but faith and a stone.

David's epic win was more than just a battle victory; it was a monumental boost for Israel's morale and a clear demonstration that courage and faith are the ultimate game-changers.

Why It Matters Today

David's showdown with Goliath hits close to home when you think about the giants you face today—be it bullying, self-doubt, or the pressure to fit in. Like David, you might feel like you're not equipped or that you're being underestimated.

This story pumps you up to tackle challenges with guts and to believe in your own unique strengths. Sometimes, like David ditching the armor for his sling, going against the grain or choosing the less obvious path can set you up for the win.

Every time you stand up for what's right, push against the odds, or stay true to your values despite the pressure, you're channeling a bit of David's spirit. You're proving that with the right mix of courage and faith, no challenge is too big to take on.

CHAPTER 23
KING SOLOMON'S WISDOM:
A GIFT AND A TEST

(1 Kings 3)

Solomon, freshly crowned as king of Israel, was feeling the pressure of his new gig. Aware of his greenness and the complexity of leading a nation, he sought some celestial backup. At Gibeon, where he offered a whopping thousand burnt offerings, God popped up in a dream, offering him a once-in-a-lifetime deal.

God to Solomon: "What do you want from me? Just name it." (1 Kings 3:5)

Solomon's answer showed he wasn't just about the bling or the power. He wanted the chops to lead right.

Solomon: "Hook me up with a discerning heart to govern your people well and to know the difference between right and wrong. Who's really up to ruling this awesome crowd of yours?" (1 Kings 3:9)

God was all in with Solomon's unselfish vibe. He blessed him with mad wisdom, plus a side of riches and honors unmatched by any king of his time. And if Solomon kept on the straight and narrow, following God's commands, he was promised a long life.

Soon enough, Solomon's new wisdom was put to the test in a drama that turned legendary. Two women, both claiming to be the mom of one baby boy, brought their case before him. It was a sticky situation with no easy outs, as there were no witnesses to back up either story.

The women shared a house and had delivered their babies around the same time. One child sadly didn't make it, and now each claimed the surviving son as her own.

First Woman: "Your honor, we live under the same roof. I had my baby with her around. She accidentally smothered her son in her sleep. Then she swapped the kids while I was out. That dead baby is hers, and the living one is mine."

Second Woman: "No way! The live one is mine, and the dead one is hers!"

Solomon listened up, then called for a sword, ready to drop a controversial solution to see the real mom's colors.

Solomon: "Chop the living kid in two and give half to each woman."

The real mom's heart went zero to a hundred, and she instantly cried out for her son's life, ready to lose him if it meant he lived.

True Mother: "Please, just give her the baby. Don't kill him!"

The other lady? She was ice cold.

Other Woman: "Neither of us gets him. Split him up!"

That's when Solomon played his hand.

Solomon: "Stop! Don't harm the kid. Give him to the first woman. She's his real mom."

Why It Matters Today

Solomon's savvy shows the deep impact wisdom and integrity have on leadership. For you today, this tale highlights the importance of seeking out wisdom and moral clarity, no matter if it's about personal choices, school challenges, or relationships.

Being able to sniff out the truth and make solid decisions is a killer skill, anytime, anywhere. Solomon's story pumps you up to chase knowledge and understanding in all you do, recognizing that real wisdom often means rolling with compassion, insight, and the guts to do right.

This retelling of Solomon's wise judgment is a prime example of how being sharp can sort out messes and uncover the real deal, encouraging you to sharpen these skills in your own life.

Chapter 24
Elijah and the Prophets
of Baal: A Test of Faith

(1 Kings 18)

During a brutal famine in Israel, tensions between the prophet Elijah and King Ahab, who had turned the people towards the worship of Baal, reached a boiling point. Elijah stepped up with a bold challenge—a showdown on Mount Carmel to settle once and for all whose god was real: Yahweh or Baal.

Elijah to Ahab: "Round up everyone in Israel and meet me on Mount Carmel. And don't forget to bring those 450 prophets of Baal and the 400 prophets of Asherah who chill at Jezebel's place." (1 Kings 18:19)

On the mountain, Elijah threw down the gauntlet to the Israelites, setting up a contest that would leave no doubts about who was God.

Elijah to the people: "How long are you gonna flip-flop between two opinions? If the Lord is God, follow Him; but if Baal, then follow him." (1 Kings 18:21)

The prophets of Baal went first. They prepared their bull and started their rituals—shouting, dancing around the altar, hoping for a divine spark. Nothing happened.

Elijah couldn't help but throw some shade:

Elijah: "Maybe shout louder? He could be thinking, or busy, or out traveling. Maybe he's asleep and needs to be woken up!" (1 Kings 18:27)

But no matter how hard they tried, Baal was MIA.

Then it was Elijah's turn. He fixed up the broken-down altar of the Lord, built a trench around it, arranged the wood, and laid the cut-up bull on top. To make his point even clearer, he soaked the whole setup with water, three times, until the trench was overflowing.

Elijah's prayer: "Lord, the God of Abraham, Isaac, and Israel, let's make it clear today that you're the boss here and that I'm your guy. Answer me, so these people will know that you, Lord, are God, and that you're turning their hearts back again." (1 Kings 18:36-37)

Instantly, fire from the Lord zapped down, consuming the sacrifice, wood, stones, soil, and all the water. The crowd was floored.

Seeing this, everyone hit the deck, shouting that Yahweh was indeed the true God.

Fired up by this win, Elijah didn't slow down. He rounded up the prophets of Baal and took them down to the Kishon Valley where he dealt with them. Then, he told Ahab that rain was about to break the drought. Soon enough, a small cloud appeared, and before long, it poured, soaking the parched land and reinforcing the might and mercy of God.

Why It Matters Today

Elijah's face-off with the prophets of Baal isn't just an epic tale of divine fireworks; it's about sticking to your guns even when you're outnumbered or unpopular. For you today, it's a call to stand firm in your beliefs, resisting peer pressure and the lure of following the crowd when it goes against what you know is right.

This story also hits on the power of showing the real deal—making decisions based on solid evidence instead of just going with the flow. It challenges you to dig deep for the truth and to be a voice for what's right and fair in your circle.

Elijah's dramatic showdown, packed with action and a clear display of truth, is a powerful reminder of how much impact one person can have when they're brave enough to stand up for what they believe in, making it a stellar story for firing up conviction and leadership in challenging times.

CHAPTER 25
DANIEL'S STAND:
COURAGE IN THE DEN

(Daniel 6)

In the mighty kingdom of Babylon, Daniel, a standout young man blessed with deep faith and sharp wit, won favor not just with God but also with the kings he served. His standout character landed him a top job under King Darius, overseeing the kingdom. However, this gig stirred up a bunch of jealousy among other officials who couldn't find any dirt on him because Daniel was all about integrity.

Conspirators: "We'll never pin anything on this guy Daniel unless it's about his faith in his God." (Daniel 6:5)

Driven by envy, these officials cooked up a plan. They got King Darius to make a rule that for the next thirty days, anyone caught praying to any god or person other than the king would be tossed into the lion's den. Darius, not seeing the trap laid for Daniel, went along and signed off on it.

King Darius: "Pray to anyone but me, and it's the lion's den for you." (Daniel 6:7)

Daniel, true to his faith, kept up his routine of praying three times a day, windows open, not hiding his devotion despite knowing the risks.

Daniel: "My God, whom I serve, deliver me and guide my path." (Daniel 6:10 - paraphrased for narrative)

Sure enough, his enemies caught him praying and dragged him before the king. Darius, regretting his decree but bound by the laws of the Medes and Persians, had no choice but to order Daniel into the den.

King Darius to Daniel: "I hope your God, whom you're always serving, can save you!" (Daniel 6:16)

A stone sealed the den, and a worried Darius spent a night fasting, hoping against hope for Daniel's safety. At the first light, he rushed to the den, calling out to see if Daniel had somehow survived.

King Darius: "Daniel, servant of the living God, did your God save you from the lions?" (Daniel 6:20)

From inside the den, Daniel's voice came through, steady and peaceful:

Daniel: "My king, live forever! God sent his angel to shut the lions' mouths. They haven't hurt me because I was found innocent in His eyes. I've done no wrong before you either, Your Majesty." (Daniel 6:21-22)

Thrilled, Darius had Daniel lifted out of the den, untouched by the lions, his faith having saved him. The schemers who set him up were thrown into the den themselves, meeting the grim fate they had planned for Daniel.

Why It Matters Today

Daniel's epic showdown in the lion's den is a powerful beacon of integrity and the guts to stand by your beliefs, even when the heat's on. As a teen, you'll face times when your principles are put to the test—whether it's bucking peer pressure or sticking to the truth when lying feels easier.

Like Daniel, staying true to your values might sometimes feel like facing lions. Opting for the popular choice might seem tempting, but Daniel's faith during his tough time didn't just see him through—it also made a massive impact on those around him, including the king.

When you're up against your own 'lions,' remember that real courage and sticking to your guns can not only pull you through but can also inspire those around you. Just like Daniel became a legend of faith and bravery, you too can be a force for good in your school, among your pals, or in your community.

YOU CAN HELP MORE TEENS INCREASE THEIR FAITH THROUGH BIBLE STORIES

Your Review Can Make a Difference!

Thank you for choosing our Bible story book for teens! We hope these stories have not only entertained but also inspired your teen to connect more deeply with their faith and understand the timeless wisdom of the Bible. Now, we need your help to share this message with more families.

Why Your Review Matters

» Spread the Word: Your review helps other parents discover a resource that can positively impact their teens' spiritual journey.

» Support Our Mission: We believe that helping teens connect with God through relatable and engaging stories is crucial. Your feedback supports this mission.

» Encourage Goodness: Leaving a review is a small act of kindness that can have a big impact, helping others find a book that brings them closer to their faith.

How to Leave a Review

» Reflect on Your Experience: Think about how the stories have resonated with your teen and any positive changes you've noticed.

» Be Honest and Specific: Share what you loved about the book and how it helped your teen understand and relate to the Bible.

» Encourage Others: Let other parents know why this book is a valuable addition to their teens' lives.

» <u>Leave 5 Stars!</u> If for any reason you did not like our book, please dont leave a review and instead email us at biblestoriesforteens@gmail.com

Share the Love, Spread the Faith

We believe that every review is a step towards helping more teens find a meaningful connection with God. Your voice can make a difference!

 <<< Leave a review on Amazon:
https://geni.us/GenZBible

Thank you for being a part of our mission to bring the Word of God to the TikTok Generation. Together, we can inspire more teens to live a life of faith and purpose.

Blessings,

The Olive Branch Publishing House

THE NEW TESTAMENT

CHAPTER 26
THE BIRTH OF JESUS:
A HUMBLE BEGINNING

(Luke 2, Matthew 1-2)

In the bustling town of Bethlehem, overcrowded and vibrant during a census mandated by Caesar Augustus, a young couple, Mary and Joseph, searched desperately for a place to stay. With every inn filled to the brim, they were left with no choice but to seek refuge in a stable, a place meant for animals, not the birth of a king.

Mary, despite the humble surroundings, gave birth to Jesus there, wrapping Him in cloths and placing Him in a manger because there was no crib available.

That night, the skies above Bethlehem lit up with an otherworldly glow as angels appeared to shepherds in the nearby fields.

Angel: "Do not be afraid. I bring you good news that will cause great joy for all the people. Today in the town of David a Savior has been born to you; he is the Messiah, the Lord." (Luke 2:10-11)

Awed and inspired, the shepherds debated briefly before deciding to see this miracle for themselves.

Shepherd 1: "Let's go to Bethlehem and see this thing that has happened, which the Lord has told us about."

Finding Mary, Joseph, and the baby Jesus just as the angels had described, their hearts were filled with joy, and they spread the word of this miraculous birth.

Meanwhile, wise men from the East, guided by a celestial star, traveled to Jerusalem seeking the newborn king.

Wise Man: "Where is the one who has been born king of the Jews? We saw his star when it rose and have come to worship him." (Matthew 2:2)

Following the star to Bethlehem, they found Jesus with Mary, and overwhelmed with reverence, they bowed down and worshiped Him, offering gifts of gold, frankincense, and myrrh.

Why It Matters Today

The birth of Jesus is like the ultimate underdog story that shows us that true greatness doesn't always start in the spotlight. Imagine, the future king not showing up in a palace, but in a stable among animals! It's like proving that you don't need to be born with a silver spoon to make a difference in the world.

For you guys today, this is a big deal because it says loud and clear: it doesn't matter if you aren't rolling up to school in the latest kicks or if your weekends aren't Insta-perfect. Jesus' start in that stable is a shout-out to all of us feeling low key or unnoticed—you've got potential that can't be measured by likes or follows.

So next time you're feeling down about not being at the center of the action, or if you're dealing with FOMO because you didn't make the cut for something you really wanted, remember this story. Greatness can come from the most unexpected places, and often, it's your actions and your character that light up your path, not your status or your setup. Keep it real, stay true to yourself, and let your actions speak. Just like Jesus, you can lead and inspire by being authentically you, no cap.

CHAPTER 27
JOHN THE BAPTIST
PREPARES THE WAY

(Mark 1, Matthew 3)

In the rugged wilderness of Judea, John the Baptist stood out not only because of his unconventional attire of camel's hair and a leather belt but also because of his powerful message that cut through the air like a sharp wind.

John the Baptist: "Repent, for the kingdom of heaven has come near!" (Matthew 3:2)

Crowds from Jerusalem and all over Judea came to hear him speak, drawn by his call for a radical change of heart and renewal. As they listened, they were moved by his passionate plea for personal transformation.

John the Baptist: "This is not just about washing away dirt. It's about preparing yourself for something huge that's coming. Cleanse your hearts, not just your bodies!"

As people confessed their shortcomings and immersed themselves in the Jordan River, John spoke of someone greater who was yet to come — someone who would not just cleanse them with water but would ignite their spirits with a fire of purity and truth.

John the Baptist: "I baptize you with water for repentance, but the one who is coming after me is more powerful than I. He will baptize you with the Holy Spirit and fire." (Matthew 3:11)

John's role was clear: he was the herald, the one sent ahead to prepare the way. His stark lifestyle and his blunt sermons stripped away the pretenses and hollow rituals that often clouded religious practices, calling everyone back to the essence of faith.

Why It Matters Today

John the Baptist's message about making way for something new and greater speaks volumes today, especially in a world cluttered with distractions and superficiality. His life challenges us to question what we fill our lives with and what we need to clear out to make space for genuine growth.

For you, John's call to "prepare the way" can be likened to decluttering your digital and social life, making room for real connections and authentic experiences. His message encourages you to strip away the unnecessary, to focus on what truly enriches your life, and to be ready for new opportunities for personal and spiritual growth.

Just like John the Baptist prepared the way for Jesus with boldness and sincerity, you too can pave your path with intention and clarity. Whether it's advocating for truth and justice, engaging in community service, or simply being genuine in your relationships, remember that preparing the way often starts with a willingness to be different and make a difference.

CHAPTER 28
THE BAPTISM OF JESUS:
A DIVINE AFFIRMATION

(Matthew 3, Mark 1, Luke 3)

On the banks of the Jordan River, a momentous occasion unfolded that would mark the beginning of Jesus' public ministry. After John the Baptist had paved the way with his calls for repentance, it was time for Jesus himself to step into the limelight, not by demanding attention, but by participating in the humble act of baptism.

John the Baptist: "Behold, the Lamb of God, who takes away the sin of the world!" (John 1:29)

As Jesus approached John for baptism, John initially hesitated, recognizing the irony of the situation.

John: "I need to be baptized by you, and do you come to me?" (Matthew 3:14)

Jesus: "Let it be so now; it is proper for us to do this to fulfill all righteousness." (Matthew 3:15)

Reluctantly, John agreed, and as he baptized Jesus, something extraordinary happened that would have been worthy of going viral today. As Jesus came up from the water, the heavens opened, and the Spirit of God descended like a dove and alighted on him. Then, a voice from heaven boomed, echoing across the waters:

Voice from Heaven: "This is my Son, whom I love; with him I am well pleased." (Matthew 3:17)

This celestial endorsement was more than just a miraculous event; it was a public declaration of Jesus' identity and mission.

Why It Matters Today

Jesus' baptism is not just a ritual; it's a profound example of humility and the importance of following God's plan, even when it seems unconventional. He didn't need to be baptized for repentance, yet he chose to identify with us, showing that true leadership involves service and sometimes following a path laid out by others.

Today, this story is a powerful reminder that you don't always have to be at the front to lead. Sometimes, leading means being part of the crowd, experiencing what others experience, and showing solidarity. It's about making choices that align with your values, even if they seem to put you in a vulnerable position.

So, whether you're deciding to stand by a friend in trouble, choosing to step back in a group project to let others shine, or following a path that might not be the most popular but feels right to you, remember Jesus at the Jordan River. His baptism shows us that true strength often comes from embracing humility, supporting others, and committing to a purpose greater than ourselves.

CHAPTER 29
THE TEMPTATION OF JESUS: A TEST OF RESOLVE

(Matthew 4, Luke 4)

After his baptism, Jesus retreated into the wilderness, a barren and isolated place where he would undergo a significant spiritual challenge. For forty days and nights, he fasted, focusing deeply on his spiritual path, preparing for the ministry that lay ahead. This time of solitude, however, would not be without interruption.

As Jesus reached the peak of his physical weakness, the tempter, known as the devil, appeared. This wasn't just a random skirmish; it was a calculated attempt to sway Jesus from His divine mission.

Devil: "If you are the Son of God, tell these stones to become bread." (Matthew 4:3)

His body weakened from fasting, the suggestion of turning stones to bread would have been enticing. However, Jesus' response revealed His unwavering commitment to spiritual nourishment over physical.

Jesus: "It is written: 'Man shall not live on bread alone, but on every word that comes from the mouth of God.'" (Matthew 4:4)

Not deterred, the devil took Jesus to the holy city, setting Him on the pinnacle of the temple.

Devil: "If you are the Son of God, throw yourself down. For it is written: 'He will command His angels concerning you,' and 'they will lift you up in their hands, so that you will not strike your foot against a stone.'" (Matthew 4:6)

Jesus: "It is also written: 'Do not put the Lord your God to the test.'" (Matthew 4:7)

Finally, the devil showed Jesus all the kingdoms of the world and their splendor.

Devil: "All this I will give you if you will bow down and worship me." (Matthew 4:9)

Jesus: "Away from me, Satan! For it is written: 'Worship the Lord your God, and serve him only.'" (Matthew 4:10)

With each refusal, Jesus demonstrated His profound integrity and commitment to His mission, not succumbing to the temptations of immediate gratification, safety, or power.

Why It Matters Today

Jesus' experience in the wilderness teaches us about resilience and the importance of aligning our actions with our deepest values. In an age dominated by instant gratification—where the next like, swipe, or purchase is often just a click away—this story invites you to consider what you stand for and what you might be sacrificing for short-term rewards.

Think about the 'temptations' you face daily: the pressure to conform, to achieve instant popularity, or to compromise your values for a quick win. Jesus' responses in the wilderness offer a blueprint for holding firm to your beliefs, even when it's tough.

So when you find yourself at a crossroads, facing choices that might stray you from your path, remember the strength it took for Jesus to remain true to His course. Like Him, you have the power to choose actions that reflect who you truly are and who you aspire to be. This story isn't just about resisting temptation; it's about recognizing that the most challenging paths often lead to the greatest rewards.

CHAPTER 30
THE WEDDING AT CANA:
A MIRACULOUS BEGINNING

(John 2)

In the small village of Cana, a wedding celebration was in full swing. Weddings in ancient times were grand events, lasting several days, filled with joy, music, and, most importantly, plenty of wine to keep the festivities lively. Jesus, along with His mother, Mary, and a few of His disciples, were among the guests, enjoying the celebration.

As the party carried on, an unexpected problem arose—the wine ran out. In those days, running out of wine was not just a minor oversight; it was a social embarrassment that could tarnish the family's reputation for years.

Mary to Jesus: "They have no more wine."

Observing the situation, Mary turned to Jesus, subtly hinting at the need for intervention. Jesus initially seemed reluctant to get involved.

Jesus: "Woman, why do you involve me? My hour has not yet come." (John 2:4)

Despite His initial response, Mary instructed the servants, showing her faith in His capabilities.

Mary to the servants: "Do whatever he tells you."

Nearby stood six stone water jars, used for ceremonial washing, each holding twenty to thirty gallons. Jesus directed the servants to fill these jars with water, and then asked them to draw some out and take it to the master of the banquet.

Upon tasting the water now turned into wine, the master of the banquet was surprised and impressed, not knowing where it had come from, though the servants knew.

Master of the banquet to the bridegroom: "Everyone brings out the choice wine first and then the cheaper wine after the guests have had too much to drink; but you have saved the best till now." (John 2:10)

This act of turning water into wine was not just a party trick; it was Jesus' first recorded miracle, signaling the start of His public ministry and revealing His glory to His disciples, who then believed in Him.

Why It Matters Today

The miracle at Cana goes beyond just an impressive party trick; it symbolizes transformation and the bringing of new joy and vitality where there was lack. It's about Jesus filling the ordinary with extraordinary meaning.

Today, this story resonates as a reminder that you have the potential to bring change and positivity to seemingly mundane situations. Whether it's turning a difficult day around with a smile, helping a friend through a tough time, or bringing new ideas and energy to a group project, you have the ability to transform your surroundings for the better.

Moreover, this story encourages you to believe in the unexpected and to find hope even in situations that seem depleted or hopeless. Just as Jesus saw possibility in plain water jars, you too can look for opportunities to make a positive impact, no matter how small or insignificant they might seem. It's about recognizing that with a little faith and initiative, you can bring about change that surprises and delights, just like the best wine served last at Cana.

CHAPTER 31
THE SERMON ON THE
MOUNT: A BLUEPRINT
FOR LIVING

(Matthew 5-7)

High up on a hillside, with the tranquil Sea of Galilee shimmering in the distance, Jesus gathered his followers and curious onlookers for what would become one of the most influential speeches in history—the Sermon on the Mount. As people settled on the grassy slopes, Jesus began to speak, his voice clear and resonant, offering a radical redefinition of what it means to live a good life.

Jesus: "Blessed are the poor in spirit, for theirs is the kingdom of heaven." (Matthew 5:3)

He continued with the Beatitudes, a series of profound statements that flipped conventional wisdom on its head. Instead of praising the powerful and successful, Jesus highlighted the meek, the merciful, the peacemakers, and those who hunger and thirst for righteousness.

As the crowd listened, Jesus delved deeper, challenging them to exceed the righteousness of the Pharisees, to love their enemies, and to pray for those who persecuted them.

Jesus: "You have heard that it was said, 'Love your neighbor and hate your enemy.' But I tell you, love your enemies and pray for those who persecute you." (Matthew 5:43-44)

He also touched on practical aspects of daily living, from the importance of reconciling with others before offering gifts at the altar to the dangers of judging others. His words weren't just moral directives; they were invitations to a new way of thinking and being.

Jesus: "Do not judge, or you too will be judged. For in the same way you judge others, you will be judged, and with the measure you use, it will be measured to you." (Matthew 7:1-2)

As Jesus concluded his sermon, he emphasized the importance of not only hearing his words but acting on them, likening those who do to a wise man who built his house on the rock.

Why It Matters Today

The Sermon on the Mount remains a cornerstone for ethical living and has influenced countless individuals and movements throughout history. Its call to live a life characterized by mercy, purity, peace, and righteousness challenges us to consider not just what we achieve, but how we go about our lives.

For you, this sermon is like the ultimate guide for "adulting." It goes beyond the superficial—beyond just looking good on social media or getting good grades. It's about building a life that stands firm through challenges because it's based on integrity, compassion, and genuine respect for others.

In a world where you're often judged by your latest post or the brand of your clothes, Jesus' message invites you to focus on what's truly important: the content of your character and the impact of your actions. It's about being someone who not only stands for the right things but also stands by them, even when it's tough. This isn't just about following rules; it's about leading a life that genuinely makes a difference, creating ripples of positivity and change that extend far beyond yourself.

Chapter 32
Jesus Calms the Storm:
A Lesson in Faith

(Mark 4, Matthew 8, Luke 8)

One evening, after a day of teaching by the Sea of Galilee, Jesus said to His disciples, "Let us go over to the other side." Without hesitation, they left the crowd behind and took Jesus in the boat just as He was. Other boats followed.

As they sailed, Jesus fell asleep on a cushion in the stern. Suddenly, a furious storm arose. The waves broke over the boat, so much that it was nearly swamped. Despite the chaos, Jesus remained asleep, undisturbed.

Disciples (panicking): "Teacher, don't you care if we drown?" (Mark 4:38)

Their voices filled with fear and desperation as they woke Him. Jesus stood up, rebuked the wind, and said to the waves:

Jesus: "Quiet! Be still!" (Mark 4:39)

Then the wind died down, and it was completely calm. He turned to His disciples and asked them:

Jesus: "Why are you so afraid? Do you still have no faith?" (Mark 4:40)

The disciples were terrified and amazed. Who was this man, they wondered, that even the wind and the waves obey Him?

Disciples: "Who is this? Even the wind and the waves obey him!" (Mark 4:41)

Why It Matters Today

The story of Jesus calming the storm goes beyond a miraculous display of power; it's a profound lesson in trust and faith. It teaches that fear often arises when we feel that the problems we face are bigger than the resources we have to handle them, forgetting the presence and power of Jesus in our lives.

This story is particularly resonant in moments of overwhelm— whether it's stress from school, issues with friends, or personal challenges. It's easy to feel like you're in that storm-tossed boat, especially when the 'waves' keep coming and 'winds' keep howling.

Jesus' question to His disciples, "Do you still have no faith?" invites you to reflect on where you place your trust when the going gets tough. It's about remembering that no problem is too big when you have faith, whether that faith is in a higher power, in the support of loved ones, or in your own resilience.

So next time you find yourself feeling swamped by life's storms, recall this moment on the Sea of Galilee. Remember that having faith doesn't mean the absence of fear, but the courage to call out and trust that you're not alone, even in the darkest of times.

CHAPTER 33
THE FEEDING OF THE 5000:
A MIRACLE OF ABUNDANCE

(*John 6, Matthew 14, Mark 6, Luke 9*)

On a day filled with teaching and healing, a great crowd had followed Jesus to a remote place near the Sea of Galilee. As the day wore on, the issue of feeding the multitude became pressing. The disciples, concerned about the lack of food and the late hour, suggested that Jesus send the crowd away to find food in nearby villages.

Disciples: "This is a remote place, and it's already very late. Send the people away so that they can go to the surrounding countryside and villages and buy themselves something to eat." (Mark 6:35-36)

Instead of dismissing the crowd, Jesus challenged His disciples.

Jesus: "You give them something to eat." (Mark 6:37)

They were incredulous, pointing out that feeding such a large crowd would take more than half a year's wages.

Disciples: "That would take more than fifty denarii! Are we to go and spend that much on bread and give it to them to eat?" (Mark 6:37)

From among the crowd, a boy offered his meager meal—five barley loaves and two small fish. It was hardly enough to feed a few, let alone thousands.

Jesus: "Bring them here to me." (Matthew 14:18)

Jesus instructed the crowd to sit down on the grass. Taking the loaves and fishes, He looked up to heaven, gave thanks, and broke the bread. The disciples then distributed the food. Miraculously, not only did everyone eat until they were satisfied, but the disciples also collected twelve baskets full of leftovers.

Why It Matters Today

The Feeding of the 5000 isn't just a story about a miraculous multiplication of food; it's about recognizing and utilizing the resources we have, no matter how small they seem. Jesus' miracle teaches that with faith, a little can go a long way.

Today, this story can be particularly empowering. It shows that you don't need to wait until you have more—more money, more time, or more experience—to make a difference. Like the boy with his loaves and fishes, what you have right now can be enough to start something great, especially when you're willing to share it and work together with others.

This miracle also highlights the power of gratitude and giving thanks, which can transform what is ordinary into something extraordinary. Whether it's a project at school, a family responsibility, or contributing to your community, approaching tasks with a mindset of abundance and gratitude can lead to surprising outcomes.

So, next time you feel limited by what you have, remember the story of the loaves and fishes. It's a call to action to use whatever you have at your disposal and to trust in the potential of even the smallest contributions.

CHAPTER 34
JESUS WALKS ON WATER:
A STEP OF FAITH

(*Matthew 14, Mark 6, John 6*)

After the miraculous feeding of the 5000, Jesus instructed His disciples to get into a boat and go ahead of Him to the other side of the Sea of Galilee while He dismissed the crowd. After everyone had left, He went up on a mountainside alone to pray. Evening came, and the boat was now far from land, battered by the waves because the wind was against it.

In the darkest hour of the night, Jesus went out to them, walking on the water. The sight was so unexpected and supernatural that the disciples were terrified, mistaking Him for a ghost.

Disciples (in terror): "It's a ghost!" (Matthew 14:26)

Jesus (calming their fears): "Take courage! It is I. Don't be afraid." (Matthew 14:27)

Peter, ever the bold one, responded to Jesus' call.

Peter: "Lord, if it's really you, tell me to come to you on the water." (Matthew 14:28)

Jesus: "Come." (Matthew 14:29)

With that single word, Peter stepped out of the boat and walked on the water towards Jesus. But when he saw the wind, he was afraid and began to sink. He cried out to Jesus for help.

Peter: "Lord, save me!" (Matthew 14:30)

Immediately, Jesus reached out His hand and caught him.

Jesus: "You of little faith, why did you doubt?" (Matthew 14:31)

Once they climbed into the boat, the wind died down. The disciples, awestruck by what they had witnessed, worshiped Jesus, proclaiming:

Disciples: "Truly you are the Son of God." (Matthew 14:33)

Why It Matters Today

This story isn't just about a miracle; it's a profound lesson in faith and focus. When Peter kept his eyes on Jesus, he did something impossible—he walked on water. But the moment he shifted his focus to the storm around him, he began to sink.

This narrative resonates deeply, especially in times of uncertainty and challenge. It's easy to feel confident and strong when things are calm, but when troubles arise, maintaining faith can be much more difficult.

Whether you're facing stress at school, difficulties in friendships, or personal challenges, the key lesson here is about where you place your focus. Focusing on your fears will only make you sink, but keeping your eyes on your goals, your values, or your faith can help you do the seemingly impossible.

This story encourages you to step out in faith, even when the conditions aren't perfect and even when you're stepping into the unknown. Remember, it's not about never having doubts; it's about what you choose to do when those doubts appear. Like Peter, you might start strong and falter, but reaching out for support—whether from family, friends, or faith—can steady you and guide you back to solid ground.

CHAPTER 35
THE TRANSFIGURATION:
A GLIMPSE OF GLORY

(Matthew 17, Mark 9, Luke 9)

One day, Jesus took Peter, James, and John up a mountain to get away from the crowds. While they were there, something incredible happened. Jesus' appearance changed completely. His face started shining like the sun, and His clothes became dazzling white, brighter than any laundry detergent could make them.

Suddenly, Moses and Elijah appeared and started talking with Jesus about His upcoming journey to Jerusalem. The sight was so extraordinary that Peter, always quick to speak, blurted out:

"Lord, it's awesome for us to be here. If you want, I'll set up three tents—one for you, one for Moses, and one for Elijah." (Matthew 17:4)

While Peter was still talking, a bright cloud surrounded them, and a voice from the cloud said:

"This is my Son, whom I love; with him I am well pleased. Listen to him!" (Matthew 17:5)

The disciples were so overwhelmed that they fell facedown on the ground, terrified. But Jesus came over, touched them, and said:

"Get up. Don't be afraid." (Matthew 17:7)

When they looked up, everything was back to normal, and Jesus was standing there alone. As they headed down the mountain, Jesus told them not to tell anyone what they had seen until after He had risen from the dead.

Why It Matters Today

The Transfiguration isn't just a show of power; it's a key moment that shows Jesus is both human and divine. It highlighted His mission and got the disciples ready for the tough times ahead, like His crucifixion and resurrection.

For you, this story shows the importance of experiences that change us and deepen our understanding. These can be moments of insight, personal victories, or strong connections with others that help clarify our purpose and path.

It also teaches the value of listening—listening to those who have wisdom to share, like parents, mentors, or spiritual guides. Just as the voice from the cloud told the disciples to listen to Jesus, finding and listening to trustworthy voices can help guide you through your own ups and downs.

Moreover, the Transfiguration reminds us that it's okay to feel overwhelmed or scared sometimes. What's important is who you turn to in those moments. Just as Jesus reassured His disciples, you can seek comfort and clarity from those who care about you, making sure you don't face your fears alone.

Chapter 36
The Good Samaritan:
Compassion Across
Boundaries

(Luke 10)

One day, as Jesus was teaching, a legal expert stood up to test Him with a question about eternal life. The conversation quickly turned to the topic of loving one's neighbor.

Expert in the Law: "Teacher, what must I do to inherit eternal life?"

Jesus: "What is written in the Law? How do you read it?"

The expert, well-versed in scripture, replied confidently:

Expert in the Law: "'Love the Lord your God with all your heart and with all your soul and with all your strength and with all your mind'; and, 'Love your neighbor as yourself.'" (Luke 10:27)

Jesus: "You have answered correctly. Do this and you will live."

But wanting to justify himself, the expert pressed further.

Expert in the Law: "And who is my neighbor?"

In response, Jesus told the parable of the Good Samaritan. He described a man who was traveling from Jerusalem to Jericho and fell into the hands of robbers who stripped him, beat him, and left him half dead. A priest and then a Levite passed by, but both avoided the man by crossing to the other side of the road.

Then, a Samaritan, a figure traditionally despised by Jews, came upon the wounded man. Moved by compassion, he took action.

Samaritan: "Let me help you."

He bandaged the man's wounds, using oil and wine, and then put him on his own donkey. He brought the man to an inn and took care of him. The next day, he gave the innkeeper two denarii.

Samaritan to the Innkeeper: "Take care of him; and when I return, I will reimburse you for any extra expense you may have." (Luke 10:35)

Jesus concluded the story and turned the question back to the legal expert.

Jesus: "Which of these three do you think was a neighbor to the man who fell into the hands of robbers?"

Expert in the Law: "The one who had mercy on him."

Jesus: "Go and do likewise."

Why It Matters Today

The parable of the Good Samaritan is a powerful challenge to expand our understanding of "neighbor" to include not just those who live near us or those we like, but anyone in need, regardless of their background or beliefs. It pushes against the boundaries of societal norms and prejudices, calling for unconditional compassion and active assistance.

This message is crucial in a world where division and indifference often seem easier than understanding and empathy. The story encourages you to act, to be the person who stops to help, to be a force for kindness and justice in your community.

Whether it's standing up for someone who is being bullied, volunteering in your community, or simply reaching out to someone who seems lonely, the story of the Good Samaritan teaches that true compassion doesn't have limits. It's about making the choice to help and to heal, not because you expect a reward, but because it's the right thing to do. This story invites you to see the world not just as a place to live, but as a place to make a difference, one act of kindness at a time.

CHAPTER 37
THE PRODIGAL SON:
A TALE OF REDEMPTION AND
UNCONDITIONAL LOVE

(Luke 15)

In one of His most touching parables, Jesus told the story of a young man and his journey from recklessness to redemption, which hit different for everyone who heard it. The story begins with a young man, the younger of two sons, who was feeling salty about the mundane life at home and decided he wanted to flex with his inheritance right away.

Younger Son to His Father: "Father, give me my share of the estate." (Luke 15:12)

So, the father divided his property between his two sons. Not long after, the younger son got together all he had, set off for a distant country, and there squandered his wealth in wild living. High key, he was living the life—until he wasn't. A severe famine hit that country, and soon he found himself in dire need.

He ended up working for a local, feeding pigs—a job that was both humiliating and eye-opening for a Jewish man, given the cultural context. He was so desperate that he even longed to eat the pig feed because no one gave him anything.

Younger Son (to himself): "How many of my father's hired servants have food to spare, and here I am starving to death! I will set out and go back to my father and say to him: Father, I have sinned against heaven and against you. I am no longer worthy to be called your son; make me like one of your hired servants." (Luke 15:17-19)

So he got up and went to his father. But while he was still a long way off, his father saw him and was filled with compassion for him; he ran to his son, threw his arms around him, and kissed him.

Father: "Quick! Bring the best robe and put it on him. Put a ring on his finger and sandals on his feet. Bring the fattened calf and kill it. Let's have a feast and celebrate. For this son of mine was dead and is alive again; he was lost and is found." (Luke 15:22-24)

Meanwhile, the older son, who had stayed home and worked diligently, was low key salty when he came back from the fields and heard the celebration.

Older Son to His Father: "Look! All these years I've been slaving for you and never disobeyed your orders. Yet you never gave me even a young goat so I could celebrate with my friends. But when this son of yours who has squandered your property with prostitutes comes home, you kill the fattened calf for him!" (Luke 15:29-30)

Father: "My son, you are always with me, and everything I have is yours. But we had to celebrate and be glad, because this brother of yours was dead and is alive again; he was lost and is found." (Luke 15:31-32)

<u>Why It Matters Today</u>

This parable is lit because it showcases the themes of forgiveness, redemption, and the unconditional love of a father. It's a savage reminder that it's never too late to make a turnaround and that true love doesn't keep score.

Whether you're feeling like the prodigal who's made mistakes or the older sibling who feels overlooked, this story speaks volumes about acceptance and grace. It's about understanding that everyone's journey is different and that being part of a squad—like a family—means celebrating each other's comebacks and supporting each other through lows.

So next time you're feeling lost or underappreciated, remember the prodigal son's return. It teaches you that no matter how far you stray, there's always a path back to those who love you, no cap.

CHAPTER 38
JESUS & THE WOMAN
CAUGHT IN ADULTERY:
COMPASSION AND JUSTICE

(John 8)

In the bustling streets of Jerusalem, Jesus faced a tense encounter that would reveal much about His teachings on compassion and justice. A woman caught in the act of adultery was thrust before Him by the religious leaders, who were eager to trap Jesus between the laws of Moses and His own teachings of forgiveness and mercy.

Pharisees and Teachers of the Law: "Teacher, this woman was caught in the act of adultery. In the Law, Moses commanded us to stone such women. Now what do you say?" (John 8:4-5)

They posed this as a challenge, hoping to catch Jesus in a dilemma. If He opposed the stoning, He'd seem to contradict Moses' Law. If He agreed, He'd clash with Roman laws that prohibited Jews from executing anyone.

Jesus' response was not immediate. Instead, He stooped down and started writing on the ground with His finger, as though He hadn't heard them. As they continued to press Him, He stood up and addressed them with a challenge that would test their own consciences.

Jesus: "Let any one of you who is without sin be the first to throw a stone at her." (John 8:7)

After saying this, He stooped down again and continued writing on the ground. The accusers, confronted by their own shortcomings, began to leave one at a time, starting with the oldest, until only Jesus was left with the woman standing there.

Jesus (to the woman): "Woman, where are they? Has no one condemned you?" (John 8:10)

Woman: "No one, sir." (John 8:11)

Jesus: "Then neither do I condemn you. Go now and leave your life of sin." (John 8:11)

Why It Matters Today

This story is powerful because it shows Jesus' refusal to judge or condemn the woman, highlighting His teachings on mercy, forgiveness, and the importance of self-reflection before judging others. It's a potent reminder of the need to be compassionate and to offer second chances, rather than rushing to judgment.

For you, this narrative is particularly relevant in a culture quick to cancel or call out others without reflection or mercy. It challenges you to think about how you judge others and the importance of empathy in understanding the complex situations people find themselves in. It's a call to action to support and uplift rather than condemn, and to remember that everyone has the capacity for change and redemption.

This story encourages everyone to look inward and consider their own flaws and vulnerabilities before passing judgment on others, promoting a culture of forgiveness and understanding in a world that often seems divided and harsh.

CHAPTER 39
LAZARUS RAISED FROM THE DEAD: A TURNAROUND THAT SHOOK ALL

(John 11)

In the town of Bethany, a dramatic scene unfolded that literally stopped people in their tracks. Lazarus, brother to Mary and Martha, was seriously ill. Despite the urgency, by the time Jesus arrived, Lazarus had already been in the tomb for four days. The vibe was low, and the sisters were heartbroken.

Martha to Jesus: "Lord, if you had been here, my brother wouldn't have died. But I know even now, whatever you ask from God, God will give you." (John 11:21-22)

Jesus hit her with a truth that was both deep and powerful.

Jesus: "Your brother will rise again." (John 11:23)

Martha thought He was talking about the resurrection at the end of time, but Jesus was about to flex His divine muscles right then and there.

Jesus: "I am the resurrection and the life. Whoever believes in me, even though they die, will live. Do you believe this?" (John 11:25-26)

Martha, still salty from her loss but holding onto her faith, affirmed her belief in Him. Then, when Mary met Jesus and fell at His feet, showing her grief, Jesus wasn't just observing; He was deeply moved. The crowd was shook—Jesus wept openly, showing His real, raw connection to their pain.

At the tomb, a cave with a stone laid across the entrance, the drama peaked.

Jesus: "Take away the stone." (John 11:39)

Martha warned about the stench since Lazarus had been dead four days, but Jesus was focused on the bigger picture.

Jesus to Martha: "Didn't I tell you that if you believe, you would see the glory of God?" (John 11:40)

As they rolled the stone away, Jesus prayed and then called out with authority that resonated through everyone's core.

Jesus: "Lazarus, come out!" (John 11:43)

And just like that, Lazarus came out, wrapped in burial cloths, alive! The crowd was beyond lit, witnessing a miracle that turned mourning into a mind-blowing celebration.

Jesus: "Take off the grave clothes and let him go." (John 11:44)

Why It Matters Today

This story is a lesson about hope and the power of belief. It's a savage reminder that what seems like an end can just be a set-up for a startling comeback. Jesus shows us that even in our lowest moments, there's potential for a turnaround that can leave everyone shook.

This narrative hits differently when thinking about the setbacks you face—whether it's dealing with loss, feeling stuck in a situation, or just being low key disappointed about how things are turning out. It teaches that bringing your troubles to someone who understands and cares can make a huge difference, flipping the script on what seems inevitable.

So next time you're faced with a situation that feels like a dead end, remember Lazarus. Step up, speak out, and let faith lead you to possibilities that can not only change your story but also inspire everyone around you. This isn't just about believing in miracles—it's about being part of one.

Chapter 40
Jesus' Triumphal Entry: Celebration and Prophecy

(Matthew 21, Mark 11, Luke 19, John 12)

As Passover approached, Jerusalem buzzed with anticipation, drawing in pilgrims from all over to celebrate. At this high point, Jesus prepared to enter the city in a way that would fulfill ancient prophecies and declare His messianic identity in a public and profound manner.

Jesus sent two disciples ahead to fetch a donkey and its colt from a nearby village, instructing them on what to say if anyone questioned their actions. This was a deliberate act to fulfill the prophecy stated by Zechariah:

Prophecy: "See, your king comes to you, gentle and riding on a donkey, and on a colt, the foal of a donkey." (Matthew 21:5)

As Jesus rode into Jerusalem on the humble donkey, a huge crowd gathered, spreading their cloaks and branches on the road before Him. The atmosphere was electric, charged with hope and celebration.

Crowd: "Hosanna to the Son of David! Blessed is he who comes in the name of the Lord! Hosanna in the highest heaven!" (Matthew 21:9)

The term "Hosanna" was originally a plea for salvation, but over time it became a shout of jubilation and praise. The people recognized Jesus as the promised Messiah who came in the name of the Lord, yet they expected a political savior, not a spiritual one.

As Jesus entered the temple area, He looked around at everything, but since it was already late, He went out to Bethany with the Twelve. This moment of reflection hinted at the challenging days ahead.

Why It Matters Today

Jesus' triumphal entry into Jerusalem, often celebrated as Palm Sunday, marks a pivotal moment in Christian history. It was a public affirmation of Jesus' kingship in the eyes of the people, yet it also set the stage for the dramatic and transformative events of His passion that would follow.

Today, this story resonates as a reminder of the importance of understanding who Jesus really is, beyond popular expectations or cultural depictions. It challenges you to consider the nature of true leadership and salvation, which in Jesus' case, was about servitude, sacrifice, and spiritual liberation rather than political power or social dominance.

This event also encourages you to think about your own moments of entry—how you present yourself in new or challenging situations, and how you handle expectations, both yours and others'. It's about recognizing the significance of humble beginnings and the power of peaceful intentions in a world that often values the exact opposites.

CHAPTER 41
THE LAST SUPPER: A LEGACY
OF LOVE AND BETRAYAL

(Matthew 26, Mark 14, Luke 22, John 13)

On the night before His crucifixion, Jesus gathered with His disciples for what would be their final meal together. This supper, held in a quiet upper room in Jerusalem, was marked not only by deep fellowship but also by significant teachings that would become the foundation for Christian sacramental life.

As they sat around the table, Jesus was aware that His time was drawing near, and He chose this intimate moment to instill lasting lessons of service and sacrifice.

Jesus (to His disciples): "I have eagerly desired to eat this Passover with you before I suffer." (Luke 22:15)

During the meal, Jesus took a loaf of bread, gave thanks, broke it, and gave it to His disciples, infusing the act with profound meaning.

Jesus: "This is my body given for you; do this in remembrance of me." (Luke 22:19)

Then, He took a cup of wine, shared it among His disciples, and spoke of it as His blood, symbolizing the new covenant between God and humanity, poured out for the forgiveness of sins.

Jesus: "This cup is the new covenant in my blood, which is poured out for you." (Luke 22:20)

But the supper was also shadowed by the prophecy of betrayal. Jesus openly declared that one of the disciples would betray Him, deeply troubling them. They began to question among themselves who it could be, leading to a poignant exchange of looks and whispers.

Jesus (identifying the betrayer subtly): "The one who has dipped his hand into the bowl with me will betray me." (Matthew 26:23)

The identified betrayer, Judas Iscariot, left the supper early under the cover of night to set his tragic plans in motion.

Why It Matters Today

The Last Supper stands as a pivotal moment in Christian tradition, encapsulating themes of community, sacrifice, and betrayal. It introduces the Eucharist, a central element of Christian worship that commemorates Jesus' sacrifice and celebrates the mystery of faith.

This story underscores the importance of loyalty and the impact of our choices. It invites reflection on the nature of betrayal—not just as a historical act by Judas but as a daily challenge in how we treat those we claim to love and respect. The story challenges you to live a life of integrity and to recognize the sacredness in your relationships.

Moreover, Jesus' act of washing the disciples' feet, which occurred during this event, models a path of humility and service, encouraging you to put others before yourself and to act with compassion and kindness, regardless of the circumstances.

CHAPTER 42
THE AGONY IN THE GARDEN: A BATTLE OF WILL & FAITH

(Matthew 26, Mark 14, Luke 22)

After the Last Supper, Jesus and His squad—His closest disciples—headed to the Garden of Gethsemane, a quiet place perfect for reflection. But this wasn't just any night of contemplation; it was a night where Jesus faced some real, heavy emotions.

Jesus to His disciples: "Sit here while I go over there and pray." (Matthew 26:36)

Taking Peter and the two sons of Zebedee—James and John—with Him, Jesus began to feel super overwhelmed. The weight of what was coming—His arrest and crucifixion—was hitting Him hard.

Jesus: "My soul is overwhelmed with sorrow to the point of death. Stay here and keep watch with me." (Matthew 26:38)

As His friends kept watch, Jesus went a little further and threw Himself to the ground in prayer, a moment of raw vulnerability that shows just how real His struggle was.

Jesus (praying): "My Father, if it is possible, may this cup be taken from me. Yet not as I will, but as you will." (Matthew 26:39)

Despite His fears, Jesus' words were no cap—a true reflection of His commitment to His Father's plan, no matter how tough it got. Returning to His disciples, He found them asleep. They were totally missing the gravity of the moment, which had to be frustrating.

Jesus to Peter: "Couldn't you men keep watch with me for one hour? Watch and pray so that you will not fall into temptation. The spirit is willing, but the flesh is weak." (Matthew 26:40-41)

Three times Jesus went away to pray, each time coming back to find His disciples snoozing. It wasn't just the physical sleep that was the issue—it was what it represented: even His closest friends couldn't fully grasp or share in the immense burden He was carrying.

After the third time, Jesus knew what was coming next.

Jesus: "Rise! Let us go! Here comes my betrayer!" (Matthew 26:46)

Why It Matters Today

Jesus' agony in the garden hits differently because it shows Him wrestling with real fears, yet choosing to stick to His mission. Today, this story is a savage reminder that even when you're feeling low key scared or anxious about the challenges you face—whether it's dealing with family issues, school pressures, or personal doubts—you're not alone in feeling this way.

This moment teaches about the power of prayer and reaching out for support when you're feeling down. It also highlights the importance of being there for your squad when they need you, as the disciples learned the hard way. Jesus' struggle in Gethsemane shows that true strength isn't about never feeling weak; it's about how you respond when you do, choosing to rise above the challenges and stay true to your path.

Chapter 43
The Arrest of Jesus:
A Test of Loyalty and
Betrayal

(Matthew 26, Mark 14, Luke 22, John 18)

The stillness of the Garden of Gethsemane was shattered when Judas, one of Jesus' own disciples, arrived with a large crowd armed with swords and clubs. Sent by the chief priests and elders, they came ready to arrest Jesus—a moment charged with tension and imminent betrayal.

As they approached, Judas, who had arranged a signal with the authorities, stepped forward.

Judas: "Greetings, Rabbi!" and then he kissed Jesus. (Matthew 26:49)

This wasn't just any kiss; it was the signal—the ultimate flex of betrayal, marking Jesus for arrest. Jesus, fully aware of what was happening, faced the moment with calm sovereignty.

Jesus to Judas: "Friend, do what you came for." (Matthew 26:50)

Then the men stepped forward, seized Jesus, and arrested Him. In the midst of this chaos, one of Jesus' disciples reacted with a savage move—he drew his sword and struck the servant of the high priest, cutting off his ear. But Jesus was quick to rebuke this act of violence.

Jesus: "Put your sword back in its place, for all who draw the sword will die by the sword. Do you think I cannot call on my Father, and he will at once put at my disposal more than twelve legions of angels?" (Matthew 26:52-53)

Even in this critical moment, Jesus emphasized peace and surrendered to the will of His Father, underscoring His commitment to His mission without violence. He healed the servant's ear, showcasing His mercy even towards those who came to harm Him.

After this, all the disciples, overwhelmed by fear and confusion, ghosted—they all fled, abandoning Jesus in His most challenging hour.

Why It Matters Today

The arrest of Jesus is a gripping narrative that explores themes of loyalty, betrayal, and the consequences of our choices. This story is a powerful call to examine the nature of true friendship and the importance of standing by your convictions, even when it's tough.

This incident also highlights the tension between reacting impulsively and responding thoughtfully. Jesus' response to the violence of His arrest—calling for non-violence and healing an enemy—serves as a woke reminder of the strength it takes to choose peace over retaliation.

Moreover, the story reveals how fear can lead to abandonment, as seen with the disciples. It's a real talk about how crucial it is to support your squad in high-key stressful times, not just when it's easy or safe. This narrative encourages you to be the kind of friend who sticks around, who supports, and who lives out loyalty, showing that true bravery sometimes lies in choosing non-violence and steadfastness in the face of adversity.

CHAPTER 44
PETER'S DENIAL: A TALE OF FEAR AND REGRET

(Matthew 26, Mark 14, Luke 22, John 18)

After Jesus was arrested and taken away, Peter followed at a distance, right into the courtyard of the high priest. He wanted to see how things would unfold, but also was deeply afraid of being associated with Jesus now that he was in custody. This fear would soon lead to one of the most poignant moments of human weakness in the New Testament.

As Peter sat with the servants to warm himself at the fire, a servant girl recognized him as one of Jesus' followers.

Servant Girl: "You also were with that Nazarene, Jesus." (Mark 14:67)

Peter's heart raced, and his fear took over. In a knee-jerk reaction, he denied it.

Peter: "I don't know or understand what you're talking about." (Mark 14:68)

He moved out to the entryway, perhaps thinking he could escape the situation. But again, someone recognized him, and again he denied knowing Jesus. The third time, those standing around insisted, pointing out his Galilean accent.

Bystander: "Surely you are one of them, for you are a Galilean." (Mark 14:70)

Peter then called down curses on himself and swore.

Peter: "I don't know this man you're talking about!" (Mark 14:71)

At that moment, the rooster crowed the second time, fulfilling what Jesus had predicted earlier—that Peter would deny Him three times before the rooster crowed twice. Upon hearing it, Peter remembered Jesus' words, and he broke down and wept bitterly.

Why It Matters Today

Peter's denial is a powerful story of fear, failure, and the very human tendency to fall short under pressure. It's a reminder that everyone, even the most devoted and seemingly brave, can falter when faced with real danger.

Today, Peter's experience is super relatable. It shows that making mistakes, even big ones, doesn't mark the end of your story. Peter felt shook after realizing what he had done, but this moment of failure wasn't the conclusion of his journey. Instead, it was a turning point that led to growth and deeper understanding.

This narrative encourages you to face your fears and own up to your mistakes, but also to understand that forgiveness and redemption are always possible. It's a call to be honest about your weaknesses and to seek strength not just within yourself but also through connections with others who can support and uplift you.

Peter's tears reflect the pain of realizing his own weakness, but they also pave the way for healing and renewal. This story teaches you that it's okay to be vulnerable and that acknowledging your shortcomings can be the first step towards overcoming them and becoming a stronger, more compassionate person.

CHAPTER 45
THE TRIAL OF JESUS: STANDING UP AGAINST THE CROWD

(Matthew 27, Mark 15, Luke 23, John 18-19)

Jesus' trial was a whirlwind of back-and-forth between various authorities, and it ended up being a major display of how twisted justice can get when people flex their power the wrong way. After being arrested and shuffled around from the high priest to Pilate, Jesus found Himself at the center of a high-stakes drama that was more about politics than truth.

When Jesus stood before Pilate, the Roman governor, He was bombarded with accusations. Yet, He kept His cool, barely saying a word. This left Pilate both impressed and baffled.

Pilate to Jesus: "Don't you hear all these charges they're making against you?" (Matthew 27:13)

Jesus: "You say so." (Matthew 27:11)

Pilate, sensing that Jesus was not your typical criminal and feeling the tension in the air, tried to dodge the bullet. He threw the decision back to the crowd, sticking with a Passover tradition of letting one prisoner go free. He gave them a choice between Jesus and Barabbas, a legit notorious guy.

Pilate to the crowd: "Who do you want me to release to you: Barabbas, or Jesus who is called the Messiah?" (Matthew 27:17)

The crowd, pumped by the chief priests, chose chaos over calm, screaming for Barabbas to be freed and for Jesus to be crucified. It was a total flip—the same crowd that hailed Jesus now turned against Him.

Crowd: "Barabbas!" (Matthew 27:21)

Seeing the situation spiraling, Pilate literally washed his hands in front of everyone, trying to show he wasn't down with this decision.

Pilate: "I am innocent of this man's blood. See to it yourselves!" (Matthew 27:24)

Even though he tried to ghost from the blame, Pilate handed Jesus over to be crucified, caving to the crowd's frenzy.

Why It Matters Today

The trial of Jesus isn't just an ancient court drama; it's a story about standing up for what's right, even when everyone around you is on a different vibe. It shows how quickly people can switch up, influenced by loud voices and bad vibes, and how tough it can be to hold on to what's true.

Think about how often you see people following the crowd, maybe even on social media, jumping on bandwagons without all the facts, or ghosting someone because it's the popular thing to do. Jesus' trial challenges you to be woke about justice and truth, pushing you to think critically and not just go along with the crowd.

It's a call to be that person who doesn't just wash their hands and walk away but stands firm, even if you're standing alone, showing real bravery and integrity. It's about not letting others dictate your actions, especially when you know deep down what's right.

CHAPTER 46
THE CRUCIFIXION OF JESUS:
A TEST OF FAITH AND
FORGIVENESS

(Matthew 27, Mark 15, Luke 23, John 19)

The day of Jesus' crucifixion was a dark and heavy chapter in history, known as Good Friday. After enduring a sham trial and brutal beatings, Jesus was led to Golgotha, the place of the skull, where He would be crucified. The weight of the wooden cross, both physical and symbolic, bore down on Him as He walked the sorrowful path, watched by crowds—some mourning, some mocking.

As He was nailed to the cross and lifted up for all to see, the atmosphere was tense, a mix of sadness and savage satisfaction from those who wanted Him gone. Above His head, the charge against Him read, "This is Jesus, the King of the Jews." But this was no ordinary king. His crown was made of thorns, and His throne was a cross.

Jesus (while being crucified): "Father, forgive them, for they do not know what they are doing." (Luke 23:34)

This plea for forgiveness, even in the midst of agonizing pain, was a powerful display of Jesus' enduring love and mercy. The soldiers cast lots for His clothes, fulfilling yet another prophecy, while the crowd watched and the leaders sneered.

Leaders: "He saved others; let him save himself if he is God's Messiah, the Chosen One." (Luke 23:35)

Even the criminals crucified alongside Him had their say. One hurled insults, but the other, recognizing who Jesus was, asked to be remembered when Jesus came into His kingdom.

Penitent Criminal: "Jesus, remember me when you come into your kingdom." (Luke 23:42)

Jesus to the criminal: "Truly I tell you, today you will be with me in paradise." (Luke 23:43)

As the hours passed, darkness fell over the land, and the weight of what was happening seemed to pause time itself. When Jesus finally breathed His last, He cried out loudly, surrendering His spirit into God's hands, a moment that shook the earth—literally. The curtain of the temple was torn in two, signifying a new way was now open for humanity to connect with God.

Why It Matters Today

The crucifixion of Jesus is a story that hits deep, showcasing the ultimate sacrifice and the profound depths of forgiveness. It's a raw look at the harsh realities of human cruelty and the powerful force of unconditional love.

Today, this narrative is about as real as it gets when it comes to understanding sacrifice, loyalty, and the impact of our actions on others. It challenges you to consider what it means to truly forgive someone, even when they've hurt you badly. Jesus' response to His tormentors and His care for the criminal beside Him show a level of woke that's hard to grasp but so crucial to strive for.

This story also serves as a savage reminder of the power of standing up for what you believe in, no matter the cost. It's about being true to yourself and your values, even when the world seems against you. Whether you're dealing with betrayals, facing tough situations, or just feeling overwhelmed by the challenges in your life, remember the courage and compassion Jesus showed on the cross. It's a call to carry that same strength and kindness in your everyday battles.

CHAPTER 47
THE RESURRECTION OF JESUS: TRIUMPH OVER THE GRAVE

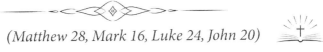

(Matthew 28, Mark 16, Luke 24, John 20)

The story of Jesus' resurrection is the cornerstone of Christian faith, embodying the ultimate victory over death and offering hope of new life. After the sorrow of Good Friday, the dawn of Easter Sunday brought a plot twist that would change the course of history.

Early in the morning, while it was still dark, Mary Magdalene went to the tomb and found the stone rolled away from the entrance. Stunned, she ran to tell Simon Peter and the other disciple, whom Jesus loved, that Jesus' body had been taken.

Mary Magdalene: "They have taken the Lord out of the tomb, and we don't know where they have put him!" (John 20:2)

Peter and the other disciple raced to the tomb, only to find the linens that had wrapped Jesus' body lying there, and the cloth that had covered His head folded up separately. The scene was bizarre—

His body was gone, but His grave clothes were left behind, as if He had simply passed through them.

Peter (thinking aloud): "What could have happened here?"

Bewildered, they went back home, but Mary stood outside the tomb crying. As she wept, she bent over to look into the tomb and saw two angels in white, seated where Jesus' body had been.

Angel to Mary: "Woman, why are you crying? Who is it you are looking for?" (John 20:13)

Thinking they were the gardener, she pleaded with them, hoping to find Jesus' body.

Mary Magdalene: "Sir, if you have carried him away, tell me where you have put him, and I will get him." (John 20:15)

Then, Jesus Himself appeared to her, though she did not recognize Him until He called her by name.

Jesus: "Mary." (John 20:16)

In that moment, everything changed. The realization hit her like a ton of bricks—Jesus was alive! Overwhelmed, she responded and soon ran to tell the disciples, who were shook by her news.

Mary Magdalene to the disciples: "I have seen the Lord!" (John 20:18)

Why It Matters Today

The resurrection of Jesus isn't just an ancient miracle; it's a story that speaks powerfully about hope and renewal. For teens today, this epic comeback story is a lit reminder that no situation is too dire for change, and no ending is truly the end.

Whether you're dealing with personal setbacks, failures at school, or challenges in your relationships, the resurrection shows that new beginnings are always possible—that you can rise again, no matter how hard you've fallen. It's about finding hope in the darkest times and knowing that sometimes, the most incredible turnarounds happen when they seem the least likely.

This narrative also challenges you to look beyond the surface and recognize the miraculous in everyday life. Just as Mary didn't recognize Jesus at first, sometimes the answers or the help we seek might be right in front of us, in forms we don't initially understand. It's a call to stay woke to the possibilities around you and to be open to the unexpected ways that new beginnings can manifest.

CHAPTER 48
THE ROAD TO EMMAUS: DISCOVERING HOPE IN DISGUISE

(Luke 24)

On the same day of Jesus' resurrection, two of His disciples were walking to a village called Emmaus, about seven miles from Jerusalem. As they walked, they discussed the recent events that had left them heartbroken and confused.

As they were talking, a man joined them on their journey. This man was Jesus, but they were kept from recognizing Him.

Jesus (to the disciples): "What are you discussing together as you walk along?" (Luke 24:17)

The disciples, looking sad, stopped and explained everything that had happened—how Jesus of Nazareth was a prophet, powerful in word and deed, who had been crucified. They expressed their hope that He would be the one to redeem Israel and mentioned the puzzling news from that morning: some women from their group had visited Jesus' tomb and found it empty. They claimed angels had told them He was alive.

Jesus (replying): "How foolish you are, and how slow to believe all that the prophets have spoken! Did not the Messiah have to suffer these things and then enter His glory?" (Luke 24:25-26)

Starting with Moses and all the Prophets, Jesus explained to them what was said in all the Scriptures concerning Himself. As they approached the village of Emmaus, Jesus acted as if He were going farther.

The disciples (urging Him): "Stay with us, for it is nearly evening; the day is almost over." (Luke 24:29)

So He went in to stay with them. When He was at the table with them, He took bread, gave thanks, broke it, and began to give it to them. At that moment, their eyes were opened, and they recognized Him. But He disappeared from their sight.

The disciples (to each other): "Were not our hearts burning within us while He talked with us on the road and opened the Scriptures to us?" (Luke 24:32)

Immediately, they got up and returned to Jerusalem. There they found the Eleven and those with them, assembled together, saying, "It is true! The Lord has risen and has appeared to Simon." Then the two disciples told what had happened on the way and how Jesus was recognized by them when He broke the bread.

Why It Matters Today

"The Road to Emmaus" is a powerful reminder of hope and recognition. It shows us that even in moments of doubt and despair, Jesus walks with us, often in ways we don't immediately recognize. This story highlights the importance of staying open to guidance and finding hope even when things seem bleak.

Life is full of uncertainties and challenges that can leave us feeling lost. This narrative encourages us to look for signs of hope and to trust that we are never alone, even when the path seems unclear.

Just like the disciples, we might not always recognize when Jesus is with us. It's important to stay open and attentive to His presence in our everyday lives, through people, events, and inner promptings.

The disciples didn't keep their encounter with Jesus to themselves. They immediately shared their experience with others. This teaches us the value of community and the impact of sharing our faith and experiences to uplift and encourage those around us.

"The Road to Emmaus" invites us to reflect on our own journeys and to stay open to the ways Jesus might be walking with us, guiding us, and revealing Himself to us in unexpected ways. It challenges us to hold on to hope and to share that hope with others, no matter the circumstances.

CHAPTER 49
THE ASCENSION OF JESUS: LEVELING UP TO THE NEXT PHASE

(Acts 1)

After the resurrection and various appearances to His followers, Jesus prepared for His final departure from Earth—a moment that was about to take things to a whole new level. Gathered with His disciples outside Jerusalem, on the Mount of Olives, Jesus was ready to pass the baton and set the stage for what was next.

As they stood together, the disciples, still buzzing with the hype from all that had happened, had one burning question left.

Disciples: "Lord, are you at this time going to restore the kingdom to Israel?" (Acts 1:6)

They were still kind of hoping Jesus might flex some royal power and set up a kingdom on Earth, but Jesus had bigger plans, a different kind of kingdom.

Jesus: "It is not for you to know the times or dates the Father has set by his own authority. But you will receive power when the Holy Spirit comes on you; and you will be my witnesses in Jerusalem, and in all Judea and Samaria, and to the ends of the earth." (Acts 1:7-8)

With those parting words, something epic happened. As the disciples watched, Jesus was lifted up, and a cloud took Him out of their sight. It was like something out of a movie—Jesus literally ascending into the sky, leveling up from His earthly mission to His heavenly throne.

Just then, two men dressed in white (angels, for real) stood beside them.

Angels: "Men of Galilee, why do you stand here looking into the sky? This same Jesus, who has been taken from you into heaven, will come back in the same way you have seen him go into heaven." (Acts 1:11)

Why It Matters Today

The ascension of Jesus isn't just about Him peacing out and leaving His crew behind. It's about passing the torch to His followers, empowering them (and all of us) to keep the movement going. It's like Jesus saying, "You've got the tools, now go build something awesome."

Today, this story is super empowering because it shows that stepping up and taking responsibility is the next level move. It's about making an impact in your own circle and beyond, using the gifts you've been given to spread positivity, help others, and make a difference.

Jesus' ascension also hypes up the promise that He's still active and involved, just in a more global, big-picture way. It's a reminder that when you're feeling low or overwhelmed, you're not flying solo—there's a bigger plan and a bigger support system that stretches beyond what you can see.

So next time you're wondering if you can handle what life's throwing at you, remember the ascension. It's a call to rise up, literally and figuratively, to face challenges with courage and to live with purpose, knowing you're part of a bigger story that's still unfolding.

CHAPTER 50
THE DAY OF PENTECOST:
WHEN THE SPIRIT CAME
DOWN

(Acts 2)

After Jesus leveled up to heaven, His disciples were left with big shoes to fill and a promise that they wouldn't have to do it alone. On the Day of Pentecost, that promise hit differently—it came to life in a spectacular way.

The disciples were all together in one place in Jerusalem when suddenly, something wild happened. It was like a scene from a blockbuster movie:

Sound Effect: "A sound like the blowing of a violent wind came from heaven and filled the whole house where they were sitting." (Acts 2:2)

Then, visual effects kicked in—what looked like tongues of fire appeared and separated, coming to rest on each of them. This wasn't just special effects though; it was real, and it was lit—literally. Each disciple was filled with the Holy Spirit and started speaking in other languages as the Spirit enabled them.

Imagine the squad suddenly able to drop bars in languages they'd never studied—Mandarin, Swahili, Portuguese, you name it. The crowd outside was shook because each person heard their own language being spoken by these Galileans.

Bewildered Visitor: "Aren't all these who are speaking Galileans? Then how is it that each of us hears them in our native language?" (Acts 2:7-8)

Peter, stepping up as the squad's spokesperson, threw down an epic sermon that cut to the heart. He didn't just explain what was going on; he connected it to Jesus' story and His recent ascension, calling everyone to take action.

Peter: "Repent and be baptized, every one of you, in the name of Jesus Christ for the forgiveness of your sins. And you will receive the gift of the Holy Spirit." (Acts 2:38)

The response was nothing short of a miracle—about 3,000 people joined the movement that day. It was a mega growth spurt for the early church, all because the disciples had the courage to speak up and the crowd was open to hearing something new.

Why It Matters Today

The Day of Pentecost is about more than just a miraculous language fest; it's about the power of communication and understanding. It shows that when people truly listen and speak in ways that reach others, amazing things can happen—barriers break down, communities form, and change is sparked.

It is a powerful reminder of the impact you can have when you find your voice and use it wisely. Whether it's advocating for what you believe in, standing up for others, or sharing your own story, your words have power. And just like the disciples, you're not on your own. The story of Pentecost reassures you that you have support—whether you see it as coming from within, from others, or from a higher power.

So next time you're in a situation where you feel your voice could make a difference, remember Pentecost. It's a call to step up, speak out, and be part of something bigger, knowing that the right words at the right time can literally change the world.

Your Review Can Make a Difference!

Thank you for choosing our Bible story book for teens! We hope these stories have not only entertained but also inspired your teen to connect more deeply with their faith and understand the timeless wisdom of the Bible. Now, we need your help to share this message with more families.

» <u>Leave 5 Stars!</u> If for any reason you did not like our book, please dont leave a review and instead email us at biblestoriesforteens@gmail.com

<u>Share the Love, Spread the Faith</u>

We believe that every review is a step towards helping more teens find a meaningful connection with God. Your voice can make a difference!

Leave a review on Amazon: https://geni.us/GenZBible

Thank you for being a part of our mission to bring the Word of God to the TikTok Generation. Together, we can inspire more teens to live a life of faith and purpose.

Blessings,

The Olive Branch Publishing House

Olive Branch
PUBLISHING

Made in United States
North Haven, CT
09 April 2025

67766369R00126